CREATING CUSTOMER VALUE THROUGH STRATEGIC MARKETING PLANNING

Creating Customer Value Through Strategic Marketing Planning

A Management Approach

by

Edwin J. Nijssen
Nijmegen School of Management, The Netherlands

and

Ruud T. Frambach
Free University Amsterdam, The Netherlands

KLUWER ACADEMIC PUBLISHERS
BOSTON / DORDRECHT / LONDON

A C.I.P. Catalogue record for this book is available from the Library of Congress.

ISBN 0-7923-7272-7

Published by Kluwer Academic Publishers,
P.O. Box 17, 3300 AA Dordrecht, The Netherlands.

Sold and distributed in North, Central and South America
by Kluwer Academic Publishers,
101 Philip Drive, Norwell, MA 02061, U.S.A.

In all other countries, sold and distributed
by Kluwer Academic Publishers,
P.O. Box 322, 3300 AH Dordrecht, The Netherlands.

Printed on acid-free paper

Printed in the Netherlands.

PREFACE

Today's commercial environment is rapidly changing. Globalization, the Internet and shortening Technology and Product Life Cycles are some of the things that come to mind. Customers seem less predictable and more critical than ever. They are looking for individual solutions and unique customer value. Consequently, understanding how to create and deliver superior customer value is essential for organizations to operate successfully in today's competitive environment. Whether your company is profit or not-for-profit, a service provider or manufacturer, a wholesaler or retailer, a business-to-consumer or business-to-business value creation is the name of the game. The key to achieving sustainable competitive advantage for virtually any organization is the ability to provide customers with an offering that is perceived to be valuable and unique. It requires a profound understanding of the value creation opportunities in the marketplace, choosing what value to create for which customers, and to deliver that value in an effective and efficient way. Strategic marketing management helps management to execute this process successfully.

This book discusses how to write a strategic marketing plan and uses an approach that is both hands-on and embedded in marketing strategy theory. The book guides the reader through the process of writing a strategic marketing plan. It is distinct from any other marketing strategy text that we know in that it briefly outlines the relevant and latest marketing strategic theory per chapter, assume that the reader is already familiar with the topic and the basic literature. Next, it discusses a range of strategic marketing management tools available per phase of the strategy formulation process. We present a selection of proven, complementary tools and discuss how they are best applied. We address and elaborate on the problems that frequently emerge when using these tools and provide practical guidelines. This approach is followed for each chapter providing the book with a clear and consistent overall structure across chapters.

The book is suitable for two purposes. First it provides students in marketing strategy with insight into how strategic marketing planning can be used to make the strategic marketing concept work. Second it provides managers with a clear framework to make the choices that are necessary to create and sustain competitive advantage; and helps them overcome specific problems encountered at different stages such as market definition, linking internal and external analyses or generating alternatives.

We have adopted this practical approach, rooted in theory, because we think that many texts fail to recognize the problems encountered when applying strategic marketing theory. They rather tell you what could or should be than what is. The books that we identified that aim to help the reader in a practical sense often over simplify things. They reduce strategy to checklists and are therefore also no help. We set out to find the right mix. The result is a short book and easy tool to help the reader address the challenging task of making a strategic marketing plan that *will* work. It provides you hands on guidelines without suggesting that making a strategic marketing plan is easy but showing you ways how to cope with the difficulties encountered.

This book has benefited from the feedback of both students and managers who have adopted our Dutch book on Marketing Strategy that was first introduced in 1995 and lived its second edition last year. The book proved to be very useful both as a stand-alone and additional reading in graduate and executive courses on Marketing Strategy at universities and other institutions for higher education as well as among practitioners dealing with strategic marketing management issues in different types of organizations. In this new international book we have adopted a true marketing perspective and focus on customer value. As such it is different from our previous work.

We welcome comments and feedback on this first international edition of our book and hope that it will prove useful in study and practice.

Nijmegen/Amsterdam, September 2000
Dr. Edwin J. Nijssen (e.nijssen@bw.kun.nl)
Dr. Ruud T. Frambach (rframbach@econ.vu.nl)

Contents

Chapter 4
IDENTIFYING RESOURCES AND CAPABILITIES FOR VALUE
CREATION: THE INTERNAL ANALYSIS

Chapter 5
TOWARDS STRATEGIC ISSUES: THE SWOT(I)-ANALYSIS

Chapter 6
CHOOSING A VALUE POSITIONING: STRATEGIC OBJECTIVES,
OPTIONS AND CHOICE

CHAPTER 1

INTRODUCING STRATEGIC MARKETING

The only thing that's certain is that the future is uncertain—especially nowadays. However, if we don't plan at all, chances that we end up where we wish to be are minimal.

--- Anonymous

1.1 INTRODUCTION

Through the years, managers and academics have tried to identify what it is that differentiates successful from unsuccessful companies. The answer lies in organizations' ability to deliver superior customer value, thus outperforming the competition in the eyes of the customer. The problem is, however, how to define and identify customer value for a particular market and how to make one's organization customer-driven. Strategic marketing is the answer. Within the boundaries of corporate and business strategy, strategic marketing is the tool to make choices regarding the customer value for a target audience. Using segmentation and positioning, strategic marketing helps to aim the company's marketing instruments to reach the market and marketing objectives formulated.

Kotler defines *Customer value* as "customers' perceptions about the benefits received from using a product relative to the costs and risks associated with acquiring it".[1] Sometimes customer value may also be defined in monetary terms. In business markets, for example, value has been defined as "the worth in monetary terms of the economic, technical, service, and social benefits a customer firm receives in exchange for the price it pays for a market offering".[2] Key in identifying opportunities for customer value is the process of analyzing the external and internal company environment. The objective is to enhance opportunities for value creation and counter threats that may jeopardize the use or power of current value generators in the future. The identification and evaluation of roads to value creation are also important as is the ability to formulate and implement plans based on the value generation decisions made. This is the challenge that marketing directors and managers are facing and what writing a strategic marketing plan is about.

To understand the process of customer value creation and write a strategic marketing plan requires knowledge of strategy, marketing and their interface. Therefore, the history and content of marketing, strategic marketing and strategic management will be presented next in this Chapter. Different schools of thought will be introduced and discussed briefly. The objective is not to give a complete literature review but rather to help the reader understand the forces that have helped shape today's strategic marketing thinking. We will show that strategic marketing evolves alongside the different phases of strategic thinking. The Chapter concludes with definitions clarifying the overlap and differences between business strategy and strategic marketing.

This introduction will provide you with the broader context of marketing strategy and will be the backdrop of the content-oriented chapters to follow.

1.2 THE EVOLUTION OF MARKETING

Everyone remembers Henry Ford's famous sentence that his customers could order his mass-produced Model T in any color they wanted, as long as it was black. It is a clear example of the *product- and manufacturing*-oriented thinking that dominated the business world at the beginning of the 20th century. This continued all through the 1930s. After World War II, however, the focus shifted. A consumption-oriented society emerged and sales became companies' focal point. The *selling concept* replaced the emphasis on efficient manufacturing and obsession for efficient manufacturing techniques. Sales effectiveness was the goal and companies' main objective was to maximize turnover. In contrast to the preceding period, management's attention was much more outward focused toward the customer. However, their intention was to sell rather than to please, and continue to please, the customer. During the late 1950s things started to change. Markets were beginning to show the first signs of maturity and saturation. New technologies and new market trends were emerging, e.g. internationalization. As a consequence organizations started pioneering the *marketing concept*, in which satisfying customer needs -those of the company's target segment in particular- were considered critical for the company's long-term financial success in the marketplace. The focus shifted from short term sales to developing and maintaining company (or brand)-customer relationships. During the 1960s and 70s *marketing theory* developed. In the 1980s and 90s it became clear that *relationships and facilitating the exchange are at the core of marketing and the marketing paradigm.*[3] After its success in consumer markets, service marketing and business to business marketing followed slowly proving that marketing was diffusing.

Figure 1.1 presents a framework of the relationships between the different business approaches. The two axis used are the level of product versus customer orientation and profit versus benevolent behavior. The first dimension refers to action, i.e. what the company does, whereas the latter concerns management's intentions and the values and norms used in doing business. The difference between the selling concept and the marketing concept now is clear. Although the selling concept may appear customer oriented, the person who is focused on sales will make a sale whenever possible, even if s/he knows that in the long run the customer may be unhappy with the product or that better options are available. In the marketing approach the idea is not so much to make a sale per se, but to provide customer value and earn customers' trust in order to turn customers into loyal customers, ensuring future sales. It may imply 'refusing' a sale and referring the customer to a better solution or competitor in the hope that this is appreciated and may result in future sales. Customer value and facilitating the exchange process by creating customers' trust and customers' willingness to invest in their relationship with the company are at the core of the marketing concept.[4]

Figure 1.1: The relationship between different management concepts

	Product oriented	**Customer oriented**
Profit oriented	Product concept	Selling concept
Benevolent	"In love with one's product"-craftsman	Marketing concept

1.3 THE EVOLUTION OF STRATEGIC MARKETING

Strategic marketing took off in the 1980s when marketing "discovered" strategic management. Until then marketing had been predominantly focused on operational decisions regarding product, price, place (distribution) and promotion, i.e. dealing with the marketing mix. However, marketers recognized that monitoring the environment and the environment-company interface was critical for the effectiveness of their operationally oriented marketing decisions. Marketers, as outward looking boundary actors, drew their conclusions and started thinking actively about strategic issues also. They embraced *strategic management* first slowly and reluctantly, then completely.[5] In the early days strategic marketing *was* strategic management.

The seminal article in *Business Week* about the death of the strategic planner that appeared in 1984 marked a change in strategic thinking in general and that of marketers in particular.[6] The article discussed the failures in strategic thinking that emerged from people at the top of the organization planning the company's strategic course separate from middle and lower management, e.g. those people in contact with the customer. The article elaborated on examples such as that from General Electric where the strategic planners at the top predicted an opportunity for smaller, energy-saving refrigerators, while sales reps reported a growing need for large machines based on the trend of one-stop shopping of double income families. The sales reps received their information from retailers in the market. This valuable information never reached the top of the organization and thus the planners. The lack of internal communication between the corporate strategic planners and sales reps caused planning failure. Therefore, the article's authors suggested to abandon the top-down "strategic planning mode" and move toward a management approach in which the strategic planning function would be integrated in line management functions. In such a model there was little or no room for strategic planners at the top or for formal plans that were not implemented. Integration and attention to implementation became the new motto.

Marketing scholars and marketing practitioners who saw this development learned from it and used it to further strategic marketing thinking. Marketers realized that they are in unique positions to influence strategic thinking in their companies. Their market research is a valuable source of information for strategy formulation. Furthermore, marketers started to use strategy to guide traditional and operational marketing decisions. Strategy was used to manage the marketing mix and make marketing decisions more robust to changes in the environment. First strategic marketers simply copied strategic management literature and thought. It was not untill the late 1980s and early 90s that strategic marketing started to differentiate itself from strategic management and started to fill the gap between business strategy and the marketing mix. It was now recognized that the gap between strategic marketing efforts and operational marketing was a barrier to marketing's further development. Since then *strategic marketing* has become *a functional strategy* that helps to accomplish and shape a company's business or corporate strategy. It has turned the focus toward market segmentation, targeting, and product and brand positioning.[7] Parallel to this development of strategic marketing specifying its own domain, a new but related topic came into vogue, i.e., *market orientation and value creation*. This topic would dominate strategic marketing thinking for the next ten years.

To improve their understanding of the characteristics of a market-oriented company, Narver and Slater and Kohli and Jaworski went back to the roots of marketing, as market-oriented companies are considered those that implement the marketing concept successfully.[8] They consulted, among other things, Philip Kotler's early work and concluded that a real market orientation requires paying attention to both customers and competitors, and gathering, analyzing and distributing this information throughout the organization. They pointed to the need for developing market information systems and adequate internal communication and information use for companies to become market oriented. They found that there was indeed a strong relationship between companies' levels of market orientation and company performance. Given the trend toward integrated electronic communication technology and knowledge management systems we can expect that building and maintaining effective market information systems, including strong decision support systems, will become more important in the near future. After the aforementioned papers, many articles have been published on the subject. Their focus has been the moderating influence of the environment and establishing key success factors for making an organization market oriented.[9]

From the notion of market orientation comes the interest in creating unique customer value. Creating a market-oriented organization is not management's ultimate goal. It is only a tool to get to better products and services for the customer, i.e. better customer value. The identification and creation of customer value based on the use of sophisticated market knowledge is what strategic marketing is about. Both corporate and business strategy provide the borders and guidelines for this value creation game.

1.4 THE EVOLUTION OF STRATEGY

Strategic management preceded marketing strategy. Therefore, understanding the evolution of strategic thinking can help to understand the evolution of strategic marketing also. The history of "strategic thinking" is next.

During the 1950s planning was mainly limited to *long term planning*. The focus was on budget allocation issues and projecting past trends into the future. There was little anticipation of change, at least as far as the company's environment was concerned.

In the 1960s and 70s things changed. Oil crises, economic recession, saturated markets and increased globalization confronted companies with change on several fronts. The planning systems that focused on budget issues and used simple projections were inadequate and needed to be replaced. Managers realized, although sometimes too late, that carefully monitoring their markets and environment and following the changes taking place was essential for company survival. From these developments implications for the firm had to be deducted in order to be able to fortify the company's strengths and to repair its weaknesses. Anticipation replaced reactive thinking and as a result *strategic planning* was born.[10]

With the introduction of strategic planning came strategic planners who spent their days analyzing the environment and formulating plans to be executed by the organization. Some managers and academics even suggested that it might be possible for firms to influence their environment (*enactment*). Planning horizons of ten or twenty years became standard practice, and everyone turned to futurologists such as Alvin Toffler and John Nashbitt who looked into their christal balls and predicted the "new world". They were popular speakers at many management seminars of those days. However, soon the limitations of these long-term time horizons became clear.

In the 1980s the cold war ended. Hardly anyone had predicted this--showing that the future is and will always be uncertain and thus that planning too far ahead does not make much sense. Therefore, managers concluded that strategic planning was probably also too mechanical. Planning horizons were limited to 3-5 years and attention shifted towards making strategy and strategic planning actually work.[11] Implementation became a new, additional focal point. The name was changed accordingly from strategic planning into *strategic management*. Furthermore, to anticipate the uncertain future, scenarios were introduced. Possible trends and developments were identified and outlined. For each of these possible future realities, management would develop a coping strategy. The idea is that as soon as a scenario becomes reality, the firm is prepared and can use it to react quickly giving it a head start over its less prepared competitors.

In reaction to the content oriented strategic management school a group of academics focussing on strategy as a process emerged. The main missionary of this school is Henry Mintzberg who suggests that strategy is about vision and feeling rather than mechanistically developed plans.[12] They think that strategy can not be planned. A *deliberate strategy* can be formulated but an actual strategy will emerge (*emerging strategy*) when management tries to implement its plans and at the same time new information and the first results of the new strategy come available.

Since the mid-1980s strategic management has been complemented by managers' interests for operational aspects of business. Total quality management, supply chain management, and just-in-time production have gained interest. New buzzwords include Business Process Reengineering and the Lean and Mean Corporation. Within some companies operational excellence has even become the focal point and has almost substituted or became synonym for strategy. Although these companies tend to be efficient, they have generally neglected their positioning. Their competitive advantage and uniqueness has often eroded leading to decreasing profitability after initial increased profitability. This danger has been recognized and generated attention lately.[13]

The *Resource-Based View of the firm* is the latest strategy school that has emerged. This school of thought builds on ideas that were first introduced in the 1950s.[14] The core idea is that companies are bundles of resources and capabilities used to derive customer value. The resources or core competencies of a company can not be imitated, substituted, or acquired easily by its competitors and the firm can use them to build its market share and to enter new related markets. The core competencies thus underlie the company's market positions and reflect its competitive advantage in the market place.[15]

The school emphasizes that companies may adapt to their environment but can also identify and thus compete in markets that fit their resources. Management guru Gary Hamel points out that many organizations copy each other or each other's strategies (i.e. evolution theory). This results in uniformity, while striving for a unique market position tends to provide more favorable results, i.e. higher rates of return. Therefore, strategy-innovation should be each company's main objective. Hamel defines strategic-innovation as an organization's capability to reshape markets resulting in new added value for its customers and stakeholders (e.g. employees and shareholders), at the same time putting off competitors by introducing new concepts and thus rules for competing in the market place.[16] Often the innovation involves strategic stretch. Excellent examples are CNN and Virgin. They both used to be small players in comparison to their competitors but surpassed them because of their high ambition and pursuit of new ideas, products and services. Especially in the case of Virgin the stretch is obvious. Coming from the music industry the company penetrated also other leisure markets such as airlines and hotels. The company accomplished this using its unique leadership, creativity, and foothold in the entertainment industry.

1.5 DEFINING STRATEGY AND MARKETING STRATEGY

The evolution of strategic marketing and strategy are very much consistent and in synchronicity. Both have increasingly emphasized the implementation aspect of strategy. However, the question remains to what extent strategic management and strategic marketing are different. The similarity lies in the attention for the fit between the company and its ever-changing environment. The difference is in the level of abstraction. Since marketing's focus is on bridging the gap between corporate or business strategy on the one hand and filling in the marketing mix on the other, it is now considered a functional strategy just like for instance the company's production, purchasing, personnel and R&D strategies. It thus has much more eye for detail. Figure 1.2 illustrates this. However, due to marketing's boundary role, the marketing function and department tend to be more involved in helping to formulate a company's corporate or business strategy than other functional areas. Traditionally marketing is closely linked with market research and thus is an important supplier of data and information (i.e. interpreted data) on the market and trends in the environment.

Strategy can be defined as the –implicitly or explicitly—chosen route by management to accomplish the company goals it has formulated, calculating for a changing environment and ensuring the fit between the organization and the environment. Corporate strategy is the corporation's overall strategic course while its different companies or strategic business units may each have their own business strategy. The latter is derived from and fits with the corporate strategy. Each business strategy again holds different functional strategies, which help it realize the business strategy. Examples of functional strategies are production, purchasing and marketing strategy. It is important that these functional strategies are formulated in line with business objectives and strategy and that they reinforce each other. *Marketing strategy* thus is a functional strategy. It is the strategy that bridges the gaps between business strategy's decisions for creating customer value and filling in the marketing mix to realize it at the customer's end. It mainly involves segmentation, targeting and positioning as well as the consistent filling in of the marketing mix instruments to create customer value in line with the general decisions made at the corporate and business levels. It covers both the content of the marketing strategy and the management of the tasks involved. However, in reality things are of course more complex and blurred. Marketing as a main supplier of market information is an important partner in the corporate and business strategy formulation process. Furthermore, as it is marketing's task to keep track of trends and market opportunities (e.g. identifying potential customers and new customer needs) marketing often leads the discussion regarding 'What business are and should we be in?' Thus like Mintzberg argues, planning is not a rigid top down process with clearly defined boundaries. It rather is a top down and bottom up process in which strategy is crafted.

Finally, we like to comment on the term *market strategy*. This is the strategy a company uses regarding the market. It is closely related to business and marketing strategy but does not so much include organizational or financial aspects. Its focus is on how the company is trying to appeal and approach customers and how it differentiates itself and tries to deal with (i.e. defend or attack) competitors.

Figure 1.2: Relationship between different strategic levels in the organization

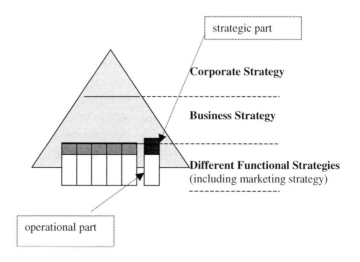

1.6 NOTES

[1] Ferrell et al. (1999).
[2] Anderson and Narus (1999).
[3] Morgan and Hunt (1994).
[4] Singh and Sirdeshmukh (2000); Nijssen, Sing, Sirdeshmukh with Holzmueller (2000); Garbarino and Johnson (1999).
[5] Day and Wensley (1983).
[6] *Business Week* (1984).
[7] E.g., Jain (1997); Hooley, Saunders and Piercy (1998); Lambin (1993).
[8] Narver and Slater (1990); Kohli and Jaworski (1990).
[9] E.g., Kohli and Jaworski (1990).
[10] See e.g. Ansoff (1964).
[11] Bonoma (1984).
[12] Mintzberg (1988).
[13] Porter (1996).
[14] Penrose (1959); Wernerfelt (1984).
[15] Barney (1991).
[16] Hamel (1998). (2000).

CHAPTER 2

DEFINING THE STRATEGIC PROBLEM

'More than anywhere else it is at the beginning of any investigation that the source of genius is to be found'

--- *Northrop*

2.1 INTRODUCTION

A sound problem definition should be the starting point of any strategic marketing planning process. The reason is simple. Knowing the company's problem is required to help management deal with it. Although this will sound logically, reality is far from simple. Generally a strategic problem does not emerge over night. It develops over time and is difficult to see and detect for people in the organization who tend to be too close and used to the problems to see them.

Managers need to look out for changes in the company environment and monitor the situation carefully to see whether the company and its activities remain contingent, providing ongoing customer value. Only this will ensure its viability in the long run. Nevertheless, a more careful problem analysis is always helpful and useful. It will help a company's management to direct its efforts by analyzing the status quo in detail and identify possible roads to future customer value while reconsidering its strategy.

Management can have several motivations for performing a strategy audit. We identify four main reasons:

1. Checking and evaluation.

A first and very common reason to conduct a strategic audit is management's periodically checking of the company strategy. Many companies evaluate their strategy on a regular basis even when there is no clear sign or reason of anything being wrong. Today's environment is continuously changing and needs to be monitored and evaluated to keep track of developments and not be caught off guard by the competition in the quest for customer value and loyalty. The level of environmental turbulence determines the frequency of and intervals between these sessions. Taking the time off to sit down and evaluate the situation and trends in the environment helps to ensure adequate strategy evolution for the company.

2. Ambition for growth.

A second reason for strategy analysis may lie in managerial ambition. In all cases where the company's development lacks behind management's ambition, we find reasons for strategy evaluation. Often this happens in a somewhat implicit way but still it involves a re-analysis of the company's market proposition and deciding on avenues for growth. This motivation is natural for small fast growing companies who consider expanding their business geographically to find new customers and companies that are looking for ways to exploit their core competencies further (e.g. many software companies and high-tech companies). Although these ambitious companies do not experience a strategic problem in the sense of having a mismatch between the firm and its changing environment, they are facing important strategic decisions. Moving into a new market constitutes a strategic problem in that a potential mismatch may occur, as the company is entering a new, and to the organization unfamiliar market. Dealing with completely new customers and competing in a new setting represents a threat of not understanding the requirements for delivering customer value or rules of competition completely. More importantly, it holds the danger of thinking one understands the rules but does not.

3. Emerging strategic gap

This third reason is probably the most common one. Companies that face a changing environment will sooner or later experience decreasing profits and market share causing the need of its management to re-evaluate the company strategy and to make important changes. The situation generally emerges when simple strategic evolution has failed but management has been alerted by symptoms (lower profits and decreasing market shares) and recognizes the need for strategy modification or reorientation (e.g. the British and French car makers, but also *Unilever* that recently abolished many of its brands). In these instances management should modify the company's strategy and redefine customer value and its value delivering processes.

4. Turnaround

The fourth and last reason for strategic analysis is when the company has really lost touch with its market and thus when a large strategic gap has been allowed to emerge. Such a manifest mis-match between the company and its environment is the result of myopia from its top management and very strong organizational inertia. Often the strategic analysis takes place after that the old top management has been removed. The result is a turnaround with a strategic reorientation and the closing down of those parts of the company that are no longer viable (e.g., *AEG*—the German electrical company, and *Fokker*—the Dutch aviation company). The reorientation requires reinventing the company's raison d'être and may take different forms. It may entail the continuation of profitable parts of the company but may also constitute a complete metamorphosis in which the company gets a complete new shape, image and product-market focus. The challenge is to determine the viable parts of the company, i.e. those parts that do or have the potential of delivering customer value for current or other markets. Examples are *Tulip Computers* in the Netherlands (from computer development and production to assembly solely), and *Digital Corporation* (some parts sold, some have become separate entities through management buy out).

These four types of motivations for strategic analysis can be captured in a two-by-two matrix (see Figure 2.1). The two dimensions refer to the presence of a potential or actual mis-fit and the need for organizational change. Although both dimensions are correlated they can best be distinguished to understand the mechanism of strategic development, i.e. the different forces at work. The position on the two dimensions determines the need for redefining the business and reconsidering the business scope.

Figure 2.1: Reasons for strategy audit

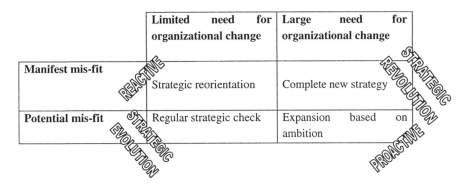

	Limited need for organizational change	Large need for organizational change
Manifest mis-fit	Strategic reorientation	Complete new strategy
Potential mis-fit	Regular strategic check	Expansion based on ambition

We can now also look at the matrix in a more abstract way. Looking at the degree and nature of change we see that in the upper left part top management has allowed for a mis-fit to emerge and that it is now reacting to the situation. Management is seriously looking for new customer value for its current customer base. In the bottom right corner the mis-fit is not yet present but is anticipated by a proactive management. The company has the ambition to grow and is actively looking to expand its scope either geographically, by attracting new customer groups or through innovation. In the lower left corner, management is considering strategic evolution, while in the top right there is a clear need for strategic revolution. In the former case the company's management is aware that monitoring its competitive situation is necessary in order to prevent decay and missing out on important opportunities to define new customer value. In the latter case the decay has reached such a state that repair of the company's competitive position is not possible. A reinvention of the company, its strategy and thus the customer value it delivers is necessary. Generally a "new" or seriously renewed company will emerge with a seriously slimmed down, more focused value creating process.

As the above suggests, in the left part of the matrix the domain of the company is definitely less likely to change than in the right part. Ambitious growth and turnaround will more seriously affect the company domain and the customer value process of the company than evolution and reaction.

There are two arguments to bring up these four different reasons for strategy auditing. First, it proves that market definition and decisions regarding business domain ("What business are we in?") are closely related to strategy formulation and evaluation. Second, it shows that the nature and scope of the strategic problems of the company together with its top management's ambition for the company determine the nature and scope of the strategic analysis that has to take place. Strategic evolution is easier and requires less attention of top management than strategic revolution. The latter will take up all top management's time and effort and even then its results will be insecure.

The question that comes to mind is how organizations become aware of strategic problems and the need for a strategy audit. It will largely be a political process of awareness creation based on an individual's notion that something is wrong or changing in the environment, and thus requires or could require management attention.

2.2 THEORETICAL BACKGROUND OF PROBLEM IDENTIFICATION AND DEFINITION

In order to be able to narrow down the problem, the organization first needs to recognize that it has a problem. However, problem recognition starts at the individual level because individuals rather than organizations perceive situations and developments. Based on this individual perception and recognition organizational problem recognition can develop. We will first address the process of organizational problem recognition. Then definitions for symptoms and problems will be provided.

Recognition

Problem recognition occurs at the level of the individual within the organization.[1] Based on certain symptoms and after a certain incubation period a change of business as usual or a strategic problem may be recognized. Often the individual will have searched for evidence and have collected data to establish the phenomenon and get a good idea about its nature. This process may involve communicating with other people inside and outside the organization about symptoms and possible causes or developments. Through internal discussion and creating political support for his or her point of view the individual will try to get the problem on the company management's agenda and recognized.

In this process three stages can be distinguished:
1. The individual or manager gathers data to get more insight into the possible problem. He or she will scan the internal and external environment using informal discussions with colleagues and contacts outside the organization.
2. The manager will interpret the data in an attempt to understand the situation and narrow down the problem often using experience and heuristics. It is important to note that in the case of a true strategic problem the functioning of the organization as a whole will be the point of discussion.
3. The manager tests his or her hypotheses by talking to other people in the organization and to find out their opinions on the subject. It concerns a rather diplomatic process in which the individual tries to gain support for his/her point of view. The objective is to get the problem recognized by the organization and create a platform for organizational action.

After that the organization has recognized the symptoms and the problem (e.g. decreasing market share and continuously high customer complaint rates), a more comprehensive diagnosis can take place. This will require additional analyses and creating further inter-subjectivity of the people involved in tackling the problem.

Except for the incremental way of problem recognition described also a more direct recognition may occur. Examples of such direct 'intervention' include the arrival of a new top manager from outside the organization or sudden pressure from outside (e.g. new entrant/competitor).

Definitions

Regarding problem identification a distinction is generally made between symptoms and problems.

Symptoms are visual or notable signals caused by (underlying) problems. They themselves are related to the problem, but are not the actual cause of strategic mis-fit.

Problems are the cause of the deviation of the situation as normal and thus are the trigger of the visual and notable symptoms.

The term "problem" generally has a negative connotation. However, it should be noted that the deviations from the situation as normal may not only refer to erosion of current roads to value creation but may also indicate the emergence of opportunities based on current company competencies. As such, we use the term "problem" to represent any (potential) deviation from present fit between the organization and its environment.

2.3 CONTENT OF PROBLEM IDENTIFICATION

For the initial identification of a strategic problem the external and internal environment of the company need to be scanned for symptoms and their possible relationship with an underlying problem. Symptoms do not so much occur in isolation but in combination. It is typically the relationships between symptoms that will help to identify the problem. As soon as we understand the structure between the symptoms we will start to understand the problem the company is facing.

Problem identification consists of three phases:

- problem identification
- stating the problem
- identifying the scope of the strategic analysis

Problem identification

We already discussed the way individuals and organizations become to recognize a problem. It is based on a process in which symptoms play a key role. Qualitative and quantitative symptoms can be distinguished.[2]

Quantitative symptoms concern the erosion of sales figures, profits, market share etceteras. Such symptoms often point to more serious problems. Qualitative symptoms concern reactions of customers or the trade. They may concern customer complaints but also information on competitor actions, possible new entrants, new technologies and economic development. Such qualitative symptoms do not have to have resulted in quantitative effects reflected in the performance measures or other indicators followed by the company's top management. Still they can be illustrative for changes in the market place and thus deviations from business as usual.

The symptoms encountered may point at different types of problems. We distinguish between manifest and urgent problems, manifest and less urgent problems, and potential or latent problems. Manifest and urgent strategic problems concern serious mis-matches between the company and its environment, such as an unfavorable cost structure during a situation of heavy competition. The market situation will put pressure on the general price level causing strong negative effects on firm profitability especially hurting those companies with an unfavorable cost structure. Severe symptoms will then be present (e.g. loss in stead of profit) and direct action will be required (to survive the potential shake out). Although manifest and urgent problems may stem from reacting to late to weak signals, they can also emerge overnight, for instance when a new technology is discovered and introduced with very short lead-time before the industry or media pick up on it. Non-manifest or latent problems can either be serious specific problems that are evolving, or general problems or trends that are "simmering". For example, the increasing professionalism and concentration of retailers has been trend for a long time. However, some manufacturers of fast-moving-packaged-consumer-goods only recognized it as a point for attention and action when power shifted dramatically in the supply chain in favor of the retailers. Firms that recognized the latent problem were able to anticipate the shifting power more successfully by creating partnerships, among others.

Stating the problem

When the symptoms have been identified they should be analyzed with respect to their interdependencies. This will create an understanding of their mutual cause and thus of the underlying problem or problems. Next this problem or these problems can be labeled. The latter will help to provide a clear starting point for the strategic analyses and narrow down the scope of the research.[3]

Too often one or a few of the symptoms are put down as "the problem" ("Our company does not meet its sales targets, therefore we have a problem"). This is incorrect and should be avoided. A sound problem definition refers to the underlying problem causing the effects/symptoms. A good definition should mention the problem and its strategic consequences, e.g., the endangering of the company's existence in the future. Consistent with our definition of strategy, a (marketing) strategic problem should refer to the link between the company and its environment. Therefore, the problem definition or description should entail a reference to the external environment and the internal environment (e.g. poorly developed marketing function * market of critical consumers and strong competitors).

Instead of a problem definition also a research question can be formulated and used to guide the process of strategic analysis. Such an approach is particularly useful in the case the strategy audit takes place based on management's overt strategic ambition (e.g., an opportunity for exporting).

Summarizing, at the beginning of a strategy audit or strategic reorientation it is best to identify the strategic problem or reason for the strategy audit/analysis. In those cases where ambition or a simple check of the current strategy is at stake a research question is a good starting point. The research question or problem definition is useful for guiding the analyses.

Identifying the scope of the strategic analysis

The problem definition or research question will guide the analysis. In the statement the problem area is identified. However, the scope of the analysis may still be open to discussion. When the borders of analysis have remained unclear or unspecified now is the time to narrow them down. This narrowing down should be accompanied by solid motivations as to what will and what will not be included in the analysis and why. The criterion to use is strategic plausibility. What do we loose by leaving something out? From a strategic perspective, a too broad scope is to be preferred over a too narrow one. In the latter case the problem will always be missed whereas in the former case it may still be found and solved.

Narrowing down the problem area is closely related to the issue of market definition. What is the company's domain and what should it be? Why do we include some markets and leave other markets out of the analysis? The corporate mission may be a guiding element. Still the rule of strategic plausible borders counting arguments for and against including something in the analyses, calculating for the quality of the arguments may be the safest way to go.

2.4 INSTRUMENTS TO USE

In order to analyze strategic symptoms and problems several instruments can be used. The analysis should lead to a document that can guide the strategic analysis. It should contain a brief description of the background of the problems that the company is facing, the problem definition (or research question) and identify the necessary scope of the analysis. The instruments are discussed in detail next.

1. *Symptom-problem scheme or causal scheme*: A simple and reliable method for analyzing problems is that of mapping symptoms systematically and tracing them back to their roots. The technique is consistent with the fish bone approach of Ishikawa. Tracing the symptoms back and relating them to each other will provide insight into the structure of the problem and the true causes of the "failure" of the organization. This approach is easy to learn and very useful. It also allows for the identification of multiple problems and setting priorities. Box 2.1 shows an example. The starting points are the most crucial points because they reflect the problems.

2. *Initial gap analysis*: This is a very crude instrument and is actually nothing more and nothing less than a global SWOT analysis (strengths, weaknesses, opportunities, threats, see Chapter 5). The gap analysis is based on a general scan of the company's external and internal environment. The symptoms are identified and linked to areas of potential matches or mis-matches between the organization and its changing environment. The benchmark is what will happen in the case that no change in company strategy takes place.

3. *Stakeholder analysis*: This method aims to systematically evaluate the organization's "legitimate" use of resources from a network and stakeholder perspective. An organization operates in a network of stakeholders. Tracing the company's key stakeholders and meeting their requirements is important for survival, but often a difficult task. Four key areas may underlie the legitimization of an organization's existence:[4]

Box 2.1: Example of causal scheme

Toy manufacturer DOLL has been making standardized children's toys since it was founded in the 1960s. The company has specialized in dolls and fluffy toys. Its management is proud of the wide variety of products offered. The company carries over 120 different regular dolls, 30 moving dolls and 20 talking dolls. Its product line of fluffy toys is even larger! It holds 20 different kind of animals and within each category some 15 or more variations (e.g., different sizes and levels of fluffiness). Retailers sometimes tell the sales reps that it is driving them crazy. With some exceptions hardly any retailer therefore carries all models. Generally only the fast movers are stocked. The other models are only sold on special request. Most retailers complain about the long delivery time. Sometimes retailers cancel their orders or withdraw before making their order, just upon hearing the expected delivery time. The general reaction is that they anticipate their customers will not want to wait so long because a birthday or special event rives the purchase.

Recently DOLL has experienced heavy competition from competitors located in the Far East. The lower wages in this part of the world and the more than acceptable product quality delivered have put a pressure on prices. DOLL has a hard time keeping up. Its sales and market share are down. And, more importantly its profits have changed in serious losses. The forecasts for next year are even worse. Therefore, DOLL's top management has decided to analyze the situation and take action. It considers focusing on the top of the market as the competition from the Far East is mainly active in the low-end part of the market. This move will allow DOLL to leverage her specialist knowledge and skills. It will also allow asking a price premium. Currently management is looking at DOLL's unfavorable inventory cost situation and delivery problems. A close look at the firm's product line seems in order. Purchasing has a hard time managing the raw materials. Both ensuring a continuous flow of raw materials and negotiating good deals with suppliers is a hassle. As the new product development department is unwilling to make any concessions with respect to design and product quality, each doll has its own set of special materials. In this matter the new product manager is supported by the previous owner and major shareholder who is still very much involved in the company although he was succeeded by his oldest daughter two years ago. Furthermore, there is the large number of small production runs. It seems that the large product variety is driving up the costs.

Below you find an attempt to capture DOLL's situation in a causal schema. The bold boxes show the main points:

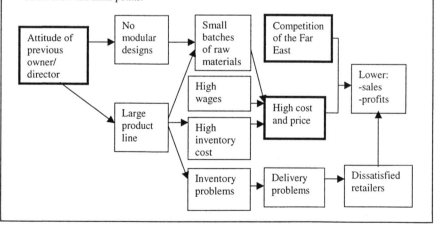

- *Market:* what role does the company play in providing products for a particular customer group, i.e. what is the level and nature of the customer value provided? If customer value is adequate the company will generate profit and remain viable. However, as soon as the company's products become obsolete, the company's future will be uncertain.
- *Funding:* for operating and making investments a company needs (working) capital. When shareholders remain absent the future of the company is again uncertain. A good example is the ".com" companies that first attracted a lot of investors but then (first quarter of 2000) became less popular.
- *Organization:* important stakeholders within the organization include employees and management. The company provides jobs and is linked to other organizations providing jobs. Institutional economics argues that this function and these links are an important determinant of survival.
- *Society:* While doing business a company has to pay attention to environmental and societal issues. If it does not do so it may face resistance from action groups and the government. Although more important for some industries than others this is something management has to calculate for.

Each of the three instruments has its charm and strengths. Consequently, some instruments are easier to use for specific types of problems and thus certain types of strategic audit than others. Below we draw a link between the tools and the different motivations for strategy auditing presented in the beginning of this Chapter. Although the choice of tool should be based on the particular situation at hand we do provide a tentative guideline.

The causal scheme method has general applicability. Drawing the figure will facilitate the analysis by supporting the manager's thinking and tracing of symptoms and problems. The initial gap analysis, however, is particularly suitable for testing a company's current strategy. It can also be applied under conditions where ambition is high. The quick scan based on a crude external and internal analysis will help uncover the main opportunities and threats and provide an initial confirmation and thus motivation for expansion. Finally, the stakeholders-approach is well suited for sensitive business problems and turnaround situations (including privatization). In industries where the legitimization of companies' business is a major issue this approach has proven to be very successful.

2.5 PRACTICAL GUIDELINES FOR EXECUTION

To conclude this chapter, we present several practical guidelines that may help execute a sound strategic problem analysis.

1. Make a list of all symptoms and analyze this list by looking for (causal) relationships. Use this analysis to track the symptoms to their original source, i.e. the underlying strategic problem.

2. Not meeting internal standards of growth or profits does not necessarily point to a strategic problem or lack of customer value. The goals may have been set too high or the performance measured incorrectly. A decrease in profitability may be logical in the light of a maturing market with higher levels of competition. A steady or increasing market share can under these conditions point to good or even excellent performance. A careful and complete analysis is thus required.

3. Make sure that the problem definition really specifies a problem. For a strategic problem this requires linking a threat to an internal weakness, or at least linking a trend in the external environment to an internal aspect of the organization (see also Chapter 5).

4. Carefully specify the market and the scope of the analysis. Make sure to motivate the focus and boundaries of the analysis well. There should be significantly more and better arguments for the point of view taken than for any other scope of analysis (e.g., when an industry is a global industry it does not make sense to limit the analysis to a specific country).

5. The advantage of a sound problem definition and scope of analysis is a more efficient strategic analysis due to a better focus. Furthermore, the initial problem definition can be used to check the outcome of the SWOT analysis later on in the process. When the final problem definition is consistent with the initial problem definition the one confirms the other and suggests being on the right track. In the case of a discrepancy between the two the manager should trace the difference. Two options come to mind. The extensive analyses have uncovered the real problem and the initial problem definition was incorrect. The initial problem definition was correct but in the extensive analysis or interpretation something went wrong.

6. The best starting point for a strategic audit is a brief document of 1 or 2 pages. It should include:

   - The background of the company;
   - The main external developments and internal weaknesses/issues;
   - The problem definition or research question; and
   - The focus and boundaries of the analysis.

2.6 NOTES

[1] Argyris and Schön (1978).

[2] Ansoff (1984).

[3] Note that the actual or final strategic problem can only be stated when the planned, more elaborate strategic analyses are performed.

[4] Based on Hoes (1985). In the original article five areas are distinguished which we collapsed into four.

CHAPTER 3
IDENTIFYING VALUE CREATION OPPORTUNITIES: THE EXTERNAL ANALYSIS

'If the dinosaurs had done an environmental analysis, they wouldn't be extinct'

---*Kevin J. Clancy & Robert S. Shulman*

3.1 INTRODUCTION

As we discussed in the previous chapter, firms may identify current problems or may foresee future problems in their ability of successfully operating in a changing environment. In order to assess the current situation in the market or broader environment and to identify future challenges that a firm's environment will impose on the organization, it is important for the organization to take an outside-in approach. Only then opportunities for both present and future customer value creation are to be identified. It is the objective of an *external analysis* to obtain such insight in both the current and future environment of the organization and to identify key success factors. The latter can be defined as the requirements set by the current and future environment which a company will have to meet in order to be able to obtain and maintain a competitive advantage in the market place.

The external analysis is an essential part of any successful strategic marketing plan. Its breadth and depth are driven by the fundamental choices the organization has made within her mission. Such mission is often captured in a mission statement that generally defines her market scope ('what business are we in?') and formulates her (growth) ambition. The company's current market scope and its ambition for growth will determine the breadth of the analysis. The more ambitious its management is the more likely that the analysis should take a broader scope in order to identify potential opportunities for growth (e.g., international markets). The depth of an external analysis refers to the quality of the insights that needs to be obtained. For example with respect to customer analysis it is important to gain insight not only in the existence and size of market segments, but to understand factors such as the needs, motives, buying behavior and communication behavior of customers within each segment. Adequate depth is thus critical to a successful external analysis and requires sound strategic market research.[1]

Although execution of formal market research may coincide more closely with the strategic planning cycle an organization should gather information on its environment and trends in its environment on a continuous basis. The organization would do itself short if the rich and potentially very useful source of information that is available on a more continuous basis such as, for example, through marketing, sales, or service personnel, would be overlooked or ignored. Scanning the market and broader environment constantly will prevent the organization from myopia and enables its management to be proactive rather than reactive. It will also contribute to the institutionalization of the external analysis changing the strategic marketing planning process from an irregular and 'strange' activity into a natural and logic way of gathering and distributing market information in the organization, making it truly market driven.

3.2 THEORETICAL BACKGROUND OF THE EXTERNAL ANALYSIS

An external analysis can be defined as an investigation into the developments within the environment of an organization with the objective to obtain insight in both the current and future key success factors within the market as well as the organization's own position.

In the introduction, we pointed out that the scope of the external analysis will be determined by the firm's market scope and ambitions. A starting point that should be part of any external analysis concerns the company's direct environment of which –in addition to the company itself—her customers and her competitors are part. This is sometimes referred to as the '3 strategic C's': Company, Customers, and Competitors.[2] In addition to customers and competitors, distributors and suppliers can be considered to be part of an organization's microenvironment. This is referred to as the *core marketing system*.[3] Michael Porter addressed the organizational competitive environment by identifying five forces that affect the organization's long term position and profitability with an industry. These forces include: incumbents, new entrants, substitute products, buyers and suppliers.[4] More recently, organizations that serve as "complementors" to the firm are identified as potentially important parties within the microenvironment. For example, in the information technology industry Intel can be considered a complementor for computer companies such as Compaq.[5] In the broader environment, we find different stakeholders, such as shareholders, financial service companies, publics, potential employees, governmental institutions, pressure groups, and the media. Finally, there are different developments at the macro level that should be analyzed. These include economic, (social-) demographic, cultural, natural, technological, political and legal developments. These developments constitute general trends for the industry which also need to be understood to anticipate shifts in the "strategy game". The organizational environment is visualized in Figure 3.1.

Figure 3.1: The organization in its environment

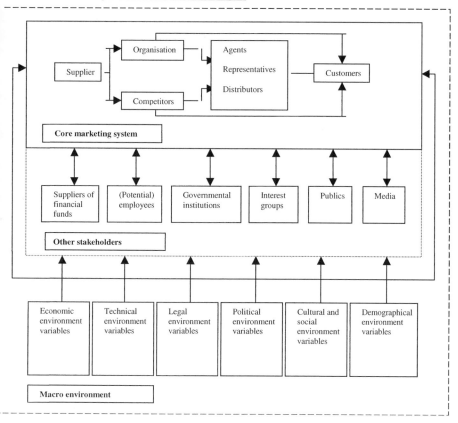

The developments that take place within the organizational environment can either be beneficial or threatening to the industry and its organizations. This depends on the extent to which these developments create opportunities to reinforce or even establish competitive advantage for companies or hurt their positions. Therefore, developments are generally categorized into opportunities or threats in order to reflect their impact on the firm's competitive advantage or its ability to sustain advantages. Here, we can observe a direct link with the broadly used concept of '*key success factors*'. The key success factors within an industry refer to those factors that an organization has to take into account in order to operate in a certain industry in a successful way. Generally they are not specific to an individual company but rather to clusters of companies that use the same strategy to reach their goals, i.e. strategic groups (more on this later).

Opportunities can be defined as events or developments that provide possible ways to create new or sustain current competitive advantages.

Threats can be defined as events or developments that erode current competitive advantage or diminish the organization's possibilities to successfully exploit her current capabilities.

An organization should thus monitor opportunities and threats in order to assess their effect on current activities and to uncover future key success factors. The latter is the ideal of any company as it may imply reformulating the rules to the strategy game and thus surpassing the competition through strategic innovation. This is consistent with the notion of *enacting the environment.*[6] Rather than anticipating or responding to developments in its environment, the organization influences the developments that are taking place or even initiates and stimulates new developments. For example, by devoting substantial resources to research on automobile safety and pollution, the automobile industry is able to influence public opinion and legislation on these issues to some extent. Enacting the environment will contribute to management's feeling of control over the environment, although such control will of course be only temporarily.

The more the environment is open to change the more uncertain it will appear and the larger the need for adequate monitoring and thus external analyses will exist. Two factors determine the degree of perceived uncertainty. First, the degree of *dynamism* of the environment contributes to its uncertainty. The more rapid developments take place, the more an organization will feel the strategic necessity to reduce uncertainties. Second, the *complexity* of the environment contributes to its degree of uncertainty. Complexity refers in this respect to the extent that a large number of forces interdependently shape the environment. In a complex environment one should not only learn which forces shape the future environment but also how these forces affect one another. Needless to say that such an environment confronts an organization with a high degree of uncertainties.

3.3 CONTENT OF THE EXTERNAL ANALYSIS

A good external analysis is aimed both at the organization's direct and its broader environment. It provides not only a description of relevant factors and their interdependencies, but analyzes the strategic consequences by taking a dynamic rather than static perspective. Thus, the degree of comprehensiveness, and by result the quality, of an external analysis is determined by three dimensions (see Figure 3.2).

First, every external analysis should include all strategically relevant actors and forces. At the very least, the analysis of the environment should consider the actors of the core marketing system, i.e. "the network of key institutions that interact to supply final markets with needed goods and services".[7] Strangely enough often, customers and potential customers are hardly touched upon in the external analysis of strategic marketing plans, although they are the backbone of any *marketing* plan. Thus, an external analysis can vary dependent on the extent to which relevant actors and forces in the environment are considered.

Second, the external analysis can vary according to the degree that the environment is actually *analyzed*. Many external analyses are mere observations and fail to draw conclusions. In an analysis, however, commonalties between and trends within the observations are identified. This results in a synthesis with respect to the status quo and conclusions regarding to the future. Based on this particularly the conclusions regarding key success factors for the firm and its strategic group are critical.

Third, the depth of the analysis can vary according to its level of detail and time scope used. Analyses can be aimed at highlighting main issues within the environment, or they can be of an extensive nature. The choice for one or the other will highly depend on the objective of the strategic analysis and the degree to which knowledge on the external environment is already present and collected in a systematic way within the firm. The analyses should be superficial regarding general trends but contain a profound analysis of crucial aspects such as consumer behavior and explaining competitors' success. In addition to the level of detail of the external analysis, the time frame used is an important aspect to look at. Strategic marketing planning is especially concerned with planning for the future. In other words it is less interested in history and historic trends then in the current situation and future predictions. Trends of the past are important to look at when they help to explain developments and make forecasts. Therefore, a good external analysis should have a dynamic character (as opposed to static) and be aimed at future trends and implications.

Figure 3.2: Dimensions of the external analysis

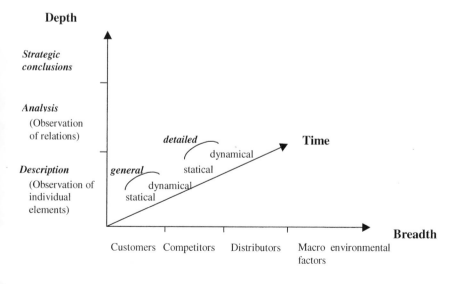

35

How to plan for an external analysis?

Before we discuss the specific instruments that can be used within the external analysis, we give some guidance on how to plan for such an analysis. Although no blueprint, the following road map may prove useful.

- Start to systematically collect information on actors and developments within the firm's environment. Classify the information according to the topic that it covers using a structure or item list as outlined in Box 3.1. Note however, that this checklist is of general nature and should be tuned to your industry.

Box 3.1: Topics within the external analysis

Market definition and general market analysis
- qualitative
- quantitative

Customer analysis
- segmentation
- analysis of segments, customer needs (benefits sought) and buying behavior
- critical success factors

Distribution analysis
- methods of distribution
- functions
- positions and value captured
- concentration degree

Competitor analysis
- competitive forces
- strategic groups
- competitor profiles
- distinctive competencies and competitive advantages

Macro-environmental analysis

For the information gathering process, use as much of the primary and secondary sources available. The first relates to active information acquisition among, for example, sales representatives by means of interviewing. The latter relates to more generally available information to be obtained through desk-research. Always write down the source of the information, as this will save time later. Note that the source tells you something about the reliability of the data. A reference to the source should accompany each table used or drafted.

- After you feel you have gathered 'enough' data, make an assessment of the relevant information obtained. Filter out as much information as possible and try to integrate it to make it easier to access. Focus on information relevant to the industry and firm and complement the information found with personal insights and common knowledge (note that this information should be substantiated later). Again using the structure outlined in Box 3.1, this will point you to blank spots in your external analysis.

- Fill in the blank spots by specific information acquisition or market research. Differentiate between critical information and 'nice to know' information. This can be done by looking at the information requirements of the different tools outlined in the remainder of this chapter. Beware that sufficient information is available on the future developments in the markets (both quantitative and qualitative information) and that all relevant aspects of the environment are covered. Make sure that the set of analyses you make captures the unique character of your industry and situation.

- For each specific area of interest within the external analysis (such as customer analysis, competitor analysis etc.), analyze the information using instruments and methods such as the ones discussed later in this chapter. Be sure to draw strategically significant conclusions from the analyses for the firms in the industry (strategic groups in particular) and the market place. High levels of detail for each separate analysis will be required to obtain strong enough conclusions.

- Based on the specific analyses relating to the different parts of the external environment, build an overall vision on how the market develops, including the implications for the firms operating in it. Focus on identifying commonalties and interdependencies within the developments.

Next, we turn to a discussion of instruments and methods that can be used within the specific analyses that are part of the external analysis. We made a selection of instruments based on our personal experience. The choice of instruments to be used should be made based on the problem and the specific situation within an industry. The instruments we discuss generally show limited overlap and thus can be used in combination.

3.4 INSTRUMENTS TO USE

In this section, we discuss different concepts, analyses and methods that may helpfully be applied to parts of the external analysis. First, we address the market definition followed by customer analysis. Segmenting the market is an important part of this section. Next, we discuss the distribution analysis followed by competitor analysis. The latter encompasses both the analysis of the competitive forces and a more in-depth analysis of individual competitors. We conclude this section with instruments to analyze the organization's macro environment.

3.4.1 DEFINING THE MARKET

A fundamental question that organizations face is 'What business are we in?' This relates to how a firm defines the market in which it operates or wishes to operate. The market definition will to a large extent determine the scope of the external analysis. In order to analyze the right market in the right way a careful assessment of the market scope that should be studied is in order.

Theodore Levitt once argued: "customers do not need a drilling machine, they need a hole in their wall". This characterizes the way in which a market can be defined. Often, marketers tend to define their market in terms of the products they market, such as drilling machines. However, this may ignore the needs that underlie customer's demand for certain products. Other, alternative products, may be introduced that serve customer needs better than existing ones. Thus, markets may be defined in terms of customer needs or value sought in order to prevent firms from becoming 'myopic' to competitors. Classic is the example how railroad transportation in the US for a long time underestimated competition from airfreight because they defined their market as 'railroad transportation' rather than 'freight transportation'.

Thus, market definitions may be based on the demand side (needs, benefits/value sought) or the supply side (products, services, attributes). The latter also includes market definitions based on identifying ones major competitors. The central question is "who do we compete with?". In this case, four levels can be distinguished that characterizes the type of competition within the market:[8]
(1) Product-form level; here the market is defined based on competition between product-forms (e.g. 'beer without alcohol' vs. 'beer with alcohol')
(2) Product category level; the market is defined based on competition between products (e.g. 'beer' vs. 'soft-drinks' vs. 'hot drinks')
(3) Generic level; competition is between generic categories of products (e.g. 'drinks' vs. 'food')
(4) Budget level; competition is between different types of consumption that customers choose between (e.g. 'drinks' vs. 'visit to cinema').

A method of defining the market that combines a supply and demand side approach, is *item-by-use analysis*. Here, customers are shown a product (=item) and are asked to indicate in which type of situations the product is or can be used (=use). Next, for each possible type of use, customers are asked to identify alternative products that can be used for each particular type of use in case the product that was shown in the first place would not be available. Thus, competitive products are identified that are considered substitutes based on the customer's desired type of application/use.

Another method that essentially combines demand and supply side aspects in defining the market is Derek Abell's market domain definition. This three-dimensional model defines the market scope and the domain that is presently occupied by the specific firm based on customer segments, customer needs and technologies that may be used to satisfy those needs. As this model can be used in a practical way to analyze customer markets, we will discuss the instrument in the next section.

In conclusion, from a marketing point of view market definitions that are based on customer needs are generally to be preferred. Needs are relatively stable over time, whereas products vary. As indicated in the above, product based market definitions may suffer from market myopia because new products and technologies become available all the time. Nevertheless, in practice we see that often more information is available on products than on customer needs. This means that in the strategic marketing plan some compromise should be made between defining the market in a conceptually desired way and defining the market in such a way that sufficient information is available so as to conduct analyses in a meaningful way.

Once the market scope is defined, an analysis of the market as a whole can be conducted. Here, one is aimed at obtaining both qualitative and quantitative information on the market. For example, market size and market growth, interesting characteristics and developments within the market and so forth. Often, secondary information will help to paint the picture. Secondary sources that provide market information may include market research agencies such as Nielsen and GfK, government institutions, organizations representing specific industries, stakeholder groups and the media.

3.4.2 CUSTOMER ANALYSIS

3.4.2.1 INTRODUCTION
By defining the market, the scope of the customer analysis is determined. This can be considered one of the most important analyses within the strategic marketing plan as customers ultimately are the central focus of every market-oriented firm.[9] Nevertheless, reality proves otherwise. In an analysis of strategic marketing plans, Clancy and Shulman found that 90% of all marketing plans discuss demographic developments, whereas only 20% provide an analysis of customer values and life style.[10] In other words, most marketing plans have only a superficial customer analysis whereas a thorough and rigorous customer analysis is important to be able to identify avenues for customer value. First, we should be aware that without a

profound understanding of the customer and his buying behavior it will be hard to identify the product and service attributes valued by the customer. Let alone that we would be able to get inspiration for innovation on how to improve customer value. Second, detailing the marketing plan (who wants what, when and where?) will be difficult without a good detailed understanding of customer buying behavior. Consequently, also marketing strategy implementation would be difficult.

The lack of customer analysis is generally caused by a lack of customer information and customer market data at within the company. How to overcome this? Secondary and primary market research can help. To what extent have the possibilities to obtain information from secondary sources (previously acquired information by others) been explored? Have all possible sources for information been reviewed and tapped? Further, has the possibility been explored to acquire information oneself or by means of a market research agency? Prime sources of information are the companies' customers, service personnel, sales representatives, and etceteras. However, other market experts can and probably should be interviewed. Performing some qualitative research is advisable. Also identifying what potentially useful documents or data are available within the organization might help. Just think of customer profitability analysis and growth figures per product line. Although these data will be biased (i.e. not representative), they may provide insight into the market and help the information gathering process. In short, firms should explore both formal and informal sources of market information and incorporate findings in the customer analysis. Such will help in analyzing the market in greater detail, for example in terms of market segments.

3.4.2.2 MARKET SEGMENTATION

We have been referring to 'the market' in general. However, within a market generally some customers are more alike than other customers. Hence, market segmentation is useful.

We define a *market segment* as *a group of customers with shared characteristics that respond to marketing activities generally in a similar way.*

Segments are defined in such a way that customers within a segment are as homogeneous as possible, whereas differences between segments are maximized. This enables marketers to target markets in an optimal way, because ideally the segments will respond to the firm's marketing mix in a somewhat different way. Therefore, market segmentation is one of the core concepts of marketing strategy. As it is the starting point for analyzing the customer market and to provide insight in customer behavior, we now briefly discuss the segmentation process.

Segmentation procedure

Within the segmentation process, three main steps need to be considered:

Choice and application of segmentation criteria

Analysis of the identified segments

Evaluate segments on attractiveness

1. Choice and application of segmentation criteria

In order to segment in a useful way, segmentation criteria need to be defined. These criteria need to be chosen in such a way that they discriminate between customers with respect to needs (including purchase motives and purchase criteria) and behavior (e.g. information search behavior and buying behavior). Only if segments are defined in this way, differentiated marketing will be possible and potentially successful.

In general, segments are subject to the following criteria in order to be valuable in marketing:

a. Segments should be *identifiable*; marketers should be able to identify the customers within a market segment;

b. Segments should be *measurable*; segment size, buying power et cetera should be measured;

c. Segments should be *sufficiently large* (to justify separate targeting);

d. Segments should be *approachable* with marketing instruments;

e. Segments should be *homogeneous in their response* to marketing activities; and

f. Segments should be relatively *stable over time*.

Segmentation criteria may vary in terms of their *observability* (age and gender are more easily identified than motives) and their *specificity* (how precisely is a segment identified by a segmentation criterion?). In industrial marketing, one distinguishes between macro-segmentation criteria and micro-criteria. The former refers to criteria that are not very specific and often observable, such as industry type and company size. The latter refers to more specific criteria that are difficult to observe, such as the composition of the Decision-Making Unit (DMU) and purchase motives of DMU-members. Criteria that are both high on observability and specificity are of course to be preferred. Box 3.2 shows some examples of segmentation criteria used in both consumer and industrial markets.[11]

Box 3.2: Examples of segmentation criteria

Consumer market
Macro:
- Geographic (e.g. country, region)
- Demographic (e.g. age, gender, household, income, profession, ethnicity, education etc.)

Micro:
- Psycho-social (e.g. Social Economic Status, life style, personality, innovativeness)
- Knowledge (cognition), Affections/emotions, Behavior (attitude, benefits sought, buyer
  readiness stage, perceived risk, loyalty, etc.)

Industrial market
Macro:
- Industry type
- Company size
- Geographic
- Production system and –technology
- Product use

Micro:
- Composition DMU
- Purchase criteria
- Culture
- Strategy

It is important to note that segmentation may be based on more than one criterion. Applying a set of criteria may help to derive more refined market segments. For example, the market for financial services may be segmented using a combination of criteria such as family life cycle, income and attitude towards financial services. This is an example of a step-wise or hierarchical approach to segmentation. The criteria are used sequentially to identify sub-segments within relative broadly defined market segments. The pre-classification is generally done using macro-criteria, while micro-criteria are used for identifying the sub-segments. Market research techniques that can be used to identify customer segments include cluster analysis, discriminant analysis and conjoint analysis.

2. Analysis of the segments

Once identified, segments should be analyzed more in depth. Both qualitative and quantitative analyses are insightful. These may include the following elements:

a. Quantitative analysis
    - size of segments
    - growth of segments
    - profitability of segments
    - customer and brand loyalty
    - etc.

b. Qualitative analysis
    - segment descriptive and characteristics
    - developments/trends
    - decision makers; decision making unit
    - purchase criteria and motives
    - purchase behavior
    - information search behavior
    - evaluation of current offerings
    - preferences
    - etc.

Detailed analysis of customer segments enables to identify the segments that are most attractive to the organization to target (step 3). It also helps to formulate more detailed market targeting plans in the strategy implementation stage of the strategic marketing planning process.

Although that the above discussion provides a guideline for analyzing customers it should be stressed that the real aim is to uncover "who buys, what, when, where and why?" Only when these questions can be answered we can start to understand "the customer" (per segment) and anticipate (new) ways of providing value and improving to these customers. To facilitate analyzing customer behavior, several models are available, specifically aimed at consumer markets or industrial markets (for references: see note [12]). Differences regarding new, modified and routine buy may also be worth looking at. The models should not be used to describe behavior but again to understand it.

3. Evaluate segments on attractiveness
Based on the detailed analysis of customer segments, their relative attractiveness to the organization can be assessed. First, the criteria to evaluate segment attractiveness have to be identified. Second, all segments are evaluated on these criteria. We will discuss this procedure as part of the portfolio analysis in chapter 4. Note that in the strategic planning process the step of evaluating and choosing market segments to target is part of the strategy selection process (we will discuss strategic choices in Chapter 6).

3.4.2.3 MARKET DOMAIN DEFINITION (DEREK ABELL)

The discussion of segmenting the market is preceded by the question of how to define the market and how to define its boarders. Derek Abell proposed a model that helps to define the market.[13] It actually identifies customer - product/technology combinations. It helps to understand the market and how customer segments, via their needs, link to the products/technologies of suppliers. To the firm it offers the possibility to explore strategic alternatives. Abell's model analyzes the market according to three dimensions. The first dimension relates to the customer groups or segments that can be identified in the market (*who* are the customers?). The second dimension addresses these customers' needs (*what* needs do they have?). The third dimension identifies the alternative technologies available to satisfy the customer needs (*how* to satisfy the needs). All three dimensions are interrelated. Based on the analysis the firm obtains an understanding of:

(a) the market in which it operates;
(b) one's own market position (by indicating what areas presently are covered by the firm, the firm's current market scope is obtained); and
(c) the alternative options that are open to the firm with respect to its served market, served needs and technologies used.

A graphic presentation of Abell's method to analyze the market and define the organization's domain is shown in Figure 3.3.

Figure 3.3: Abell's domain definition[14]

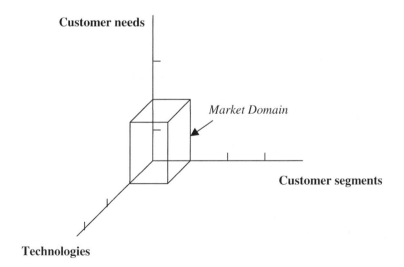

As becomes clear from the visual representation of the model, Abell's method forces the analyst to segment the market on multiple criteria. First, different customer groups are to be identified. Here, an exhaustive and mutually exclusive segmentation of the defined market is desired. This requires that prior to segmentation the market has been defined. Second, customer needs are identified that relate to the customer groups. By relating these two dimensions, a sub-segmentation of the market may be obtained. Third, alternative technologies that are used or are available to satisfy the customers' needs should be identified. Here, it is tempting to list all possible products that are brought to market to satisfy current needs. However, this may lead to too much thinking "within-the-box". First, by considering the present products that are used to satisfy customer needs one ignores future opportunities and other potentially valid capabilities to satisfy those needs. Strategic thinking requires that other than currently used solutions are explored. For example, by considering the technologies or distinctive capabilities that underlies the products rather than the products themselves. Also technologies or competencies that currently are not used yet may be represented as this reflects the dynamics in the market place. Second, products are essentially *problem solvers* targeted at specific customers, with specific needs, using specific technologies. As such, products are combinations of the three dimensions of the framework rather than part of a single dimension. As George Day notes: "a discrete product is the consequence of applying a technology to a customer need".[15]

In order for the framework to make a valuable contribution to the customer analysis, one should go beyond mere description of the market according to the three dimensions. Rather, the developments on each dimension should be explored in conjunction with the other dimensions. Tentatively, the fit between customer needs of different customer groups with alternative technologies or capabilities can be explored as well as the organization's strategic opportunities. By comparing the dynamics on the three dimensions and their interdependencies with the firm's current market domain, insight is provided in the firm's current and future strategic position. Relate your market definition to the strategic problem that you have defined earlier (Chapter 2). Also, be sure to be consistent with respect to the level of analysis in defining the different dimensions within the model. Customer segments and customer needs should relate to the same type of customers. For example, in case an analysis of both consumers and distributors is desirable, two separate models should be analyzed.

Anyone who has ever tried to use Abell's model to define a market will know that it is often not easy. Generally there are several ways that the axes can be specified or filled in leading to different pictures of the market. Some people find this annoying. However, we like to point out that this exercise is an important step in understanding the market and the strategic implications of the market definition. Only when explored and considered, a good and motivated choice can be made for a particular market definition in line with the strategic problem at hand and the strategic ambition of the company. To facilitate the market definition process it is important to consider the specific type of market in interpreting the axes (e.g. in the restaurant business we find full and self-service restaurants that provide different value to the customer -speed, convenience versus luxury wining and dining service. In this case technology is better interpreted as service process technology than product technology.)

We now turn to a discussion of analyzing the distribution.

3.4.3 DISTRIBUTION ANALYSIS

Distribution channels generally play an important role in creating value for the customer.[16] In some markets, such as fast moving consumer goods markets, it is highly dependent on the distributor as he provides the actual service to the customer. A similar situation can be seen for specialized products in the computer industry where the word 'value-added reseller' makes our point. However, we also see industries where the trade is struggling because they fail to create extra value for the customer leading to exclusion form the channel (e.g. pharmaceutical wholesalers). At the same time the evolution of new media and thus alternative channels of distributions is a hot topic creating new opportunities for companies. In this light it seems strange that distribution analysis is not well covered by many strategic marketing planning process and plans. We propose that every strategic marketing analysis, i.e. external analysis, should at least consider three topics regarding distribution, i.e. (a) channel functions, (b) channel alternatives and forms, and (c) value capture within the distribution channel. The three of them together constitute the distribution structure or help explain it. These aspects are discussed next.

a. Channel functions

The first question that needs to be addressed relates to the alternative channel functions that are or could be performed within the market that is analyzed. Two basic functions can be distinguished: the logistic and marketing function. The former relates to the logistic process through which goods are made available to customers. The analysis could focus on current practices within the market and opportunities for efficient logistics handling. Developments within supply chain management have important influence on the physical distribution within markets. For example, efficient consumer response (ECR) has changed logistics within markets of fast moving consumer goods, while mass customization affects production and distribution also. It is important to identify these developments or potential opportunities as they will effect market structure in the long run and may help redefine customer value in the market place.

The marketing function of distribution relates to the marketing activities performed by the distributors in relation to the manufacturers' products that enhance the 'offerings' value to the customer. Here, we can think of marketing tactics, service delivery (including product augmentations), in-store promotion, relationship marketing, market research and so forth. Again, the analysis here should provide insight into the extent that such functions are either currently executed or that

46

opportunities and capabilities exist to perform such functions in the future. Both customer expectations and distributors' professionalism play an important role in this respect.

b. Channel alternatives and forms

Products and services can reach the customer market in various ways. Here, both the alternatives that are presently used and that might be used define the market's structure. In general, one can distinguish between direct and indirect channels; long and short. It is important to identify potential changes that could take place in the distribution structure in the future. In this respect, it is important to consider distributors' strategies, buying motives, and buying criteria. These will include considerations pertaining to the distributor's target market, profitability targets, positioning motives, and relational and power motives. Also, it is relevant to analyze potential alternatives to current distribution channels. Electronic commerce may affect certain markets more severely than others. For example, financial service providers increasingly face issues related to multi-channel distribution where the mix between traditional channels (e.g. branches and intermediaries) with new channels (e.g. telephone, Internet) is a highly relevant topic. Thus, the analysis of (potentially available or used) alternative distribution forms aims to provide an understanding of the distribution practices and opportunities available.

c. Value capture

Third, and maybe most importantly, the strategic analysis of distribution should include an analysis of the relative share of total value that the different organizations in the supply chain capture. Again, not only the present situation should be analyzed; also shifts in value creation and value capture should be tracked.[17] This will provide insight in the relative power of organizations within the supply chain. For example, food retailers have increasingly been able top increase their share of value created in the fast moving consumer goods industry by cooperation and concentration of outlets. This not only provided them with efficiency gains and increased buying power it also enabled them to successfully introduce private label (distributor) brands.

3.4.4 COMPETITOR ANALYSIS

As strategic marketing decisions involve ways to fulfill customers' needs in a unique and superior way, it is important to understand competitive forces and competitors' ability to meet key success factors in the market place. Why are there winners and losers in the market place? What differentiates winners and losers?

The extent to which an organization is able to create and sustain superior customer value depends largely on the competing and substitute offerings. Thus, an essential part of any strategic analysis is to understand both competitive forces and competitor profiles, i.e. strengths and weaknesses. This is the scope of the competitor analysis.

A competitor analysis consists of four steps:

a. Define and analyze the structure and characteristics of an industry and anticipate competitive forces,
b. Identify and analyze strategic groups within the industry,
c. Identify, analyze and evaluate the most important competitors, and
d. Anticipate competitors' future strategies and actions.

We will now address each step and discuss it in more detail.

a. Defining and analyzing the structure and characteristics of an industry and anticipating competitive forces

By defining the market (see 3.4.1), the scope of the industry that is to be analyzed has also been defined. However, as most serious industry shake-ups occur by firms from outside the industry we should broaden our scope first and also include potential entrants and suppliers of substitute technologies. A popular tool for this, i.e. for such a broad but integrated approach of competition analysis is Porter's five competitive forces model.[18] In addition to direct competition that occurs in an industry Porter distinguishes four other competitive forces. These include suppliers' and customers' power to integrate vertically, the threat of new entrants, and the competitive power of substitute products. Figure 3.4 depicts Porter's analysis of an industry as well as the factors that determine the strengths of each of the five competitive forces within the model. The model provides us with an understanding of the level of competition in an industry and how it is derived. High levels of competition are associated with low industry profitability. Low levels of competition are associated with more favorable levels of profitability. A relationship with the concept of industry life cycle and the Porter model is present.

Although Porter's five-forces-framework is a popular and insightful instrument to analyze the competitive forces within an industry, it has been pointed out that the model is subject to certain implicit assumptions that restrict its applicability.[19] First, the model is more appropriate for industries with relatively low levels of uncertainty because under conditions of high uncertainty the forces in the model will be extremely difficult to analyze in a systematic and structured way, i.e. estimate and predict., a good example being the ICT industry. Second, the model implicitly assumes that competition is based on a win-loose situation (zero-sum game). However, in some industries competitors cooperate to create a win-win situation. Especially in case these firms can offer complementing products, such as Intel and Microsoft. Therefore, Andy Grove (Intel) proposed to add a sixth force to Porter's framework, i.e. complementors.

48

Figure 3.4: Five-forces-framework[20]

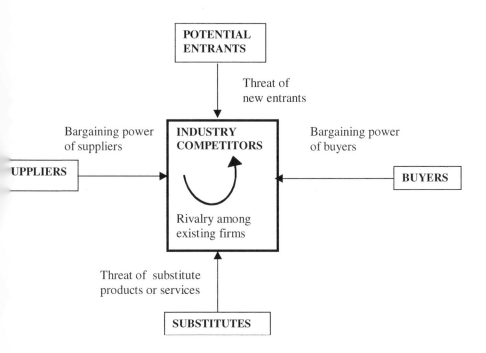

Third, the five-forces-framework assumes that sustainable competitive advantage can be gained by successfully creating barriers to entry and mobility barriers. However, competitive advantage can also be gained by customer value creating though (strategic) innovation. Strategic innovations are a "... fundamental re-conceptualization of what the business is all about, that, in turn, leads to a dramatically different way of playing the game in an existing business"[21]. In conclusion, it becomes clear that Porter's five forces model is a useful framework to understand the process that takes place in existing industries between firms to capture the value offered by the industry. Entirely new value creation through strategic innovation may be less understood by Porter's framework as whole new industries are created. Developments at the macro-level may signal the emergence of such strategic innovations, and thus of new industries.

b. Identifying and analyzing strategic groups within the industry

Once the competitive landscape has been painted, a more detailed and structured analysis of the relevant players in the industry is in order. A useful analysis in this respect is the identification of strategic groups. A strategic group is a cluster of organizations trying to reach their goals in a similar way. Consequently, the organizations within a strategic group show large similarities with respect to their strategy and thus the way in which they set out to create and deliver customer value. These strategic groups are relatively stable over time because they build their organizations, processes, and a culture in line with this strategy.

In order to identify strategic groups within an industry, the following procedure can be used.

First, the main competitors within the market should be identified. Second, by analyzing the organizations' (competitive) strategies, the main dimensions that are used to compete on within the industry are to be identified. The most relevant strategic dimensions may vary widely from one industry to another. Porter suggests strategic characteristics that could be used to assess the strategic dimensions that are a useful basis to identify strategic groups upon. These include among others:

- the degree of product or market specialization
- brand image
- push versus pull strategy with respect to the distribution channel
- distribution strategy
- product quality level
- technological leadership
- degree of vertical integration
- relative cost position
- supporting activities
- relative price level
- financial leverage
- organization structure

Third, the different competitors can be grouped according to their relative disposition on the main strategic dimensions that are identified within the industry. In practice, this may either relate to firms' Strategic Business Units or –in case an organization is primarily operating in a single market only—the entire organization. Ideally, firms are grouped on two dimensions at a time in order to facilitate the identification of strategic groups and their analysis. A two-dimensional visual representation of the firms' relative position on the dimensions facilitates the analysis; this is referred to as a strategic group mapping. Multiple representations of strategic groups may be useful or necessary to capture the strategic competitive complexity of the industry. An example of a strategic group mapping is depicted in Figure 3.5. Fourth, a dynamic analysis of the strategic groups can be executed by inferring potential and expected (substantiated by information) changes of firms' relative position on the strategic dimensions. In this way, the strategic group analysis takes on a dynamic, and therefore, strategically more insightful character.

Figure 3.5: Strategic group mapping (example)

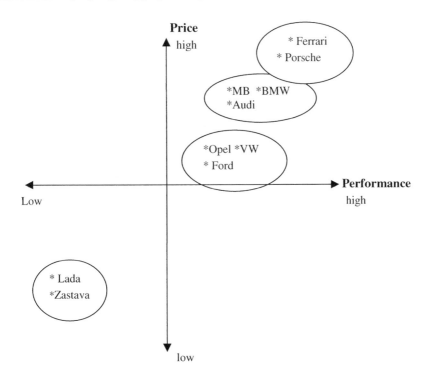

c. Identifying, analyzing and evaluating the most important competitors

Based on the strategic group analysis an organization can identify its direct, and therefore probably most important, competitors. These are the organizations that compete within the same strategic group. These firms are likely to operate on the same target market with similar strategies. In order to understand the competitors' relative ability to compete successfully in the industry, both in the present and in the future, it is important to analyze each competitor's strategic profile. Such an analysis should include an assessment of the competitors' relative strengths and weaknesses (capability profile), their goals and strategy and their assumptions about operating within the industry. The latter will help –in relation to competitors' goals—to understand potential future actions of competing firms. This is the main subject of the fourth step of a competitor analysis. The analysis of the capability profile of competitors may include the factors that will also be considered in analyzing ones own relative (dis)advantages, i.e. the internal analysis (see Chapter 4). The main objective of this competitor analysis is to find out why some firms are winners and others losers in the market place. Only when differences in competitor profiles can be identified that may explain performance differences we will have insight into what drives success in our market.

d. Anticipating competitors' future strategies and actions

Strategic thinking requires that an organization pro-actively anticipates competitive actions and reactions. In order to obtain such a pro-active understanding, the organization that performs a competitor analysis could evaluate the following questions for each (potentially) important competitor:[22]

- *To what extent is the competitor satisfied with his current market position?* In case the competitor is less satisfied with his present position, it is likely that he will follow up on market developments quickly and will try to profit from opportunities that arise in the market.

- *Which possible courses of action are open to the competitor?* Given the competitor's capability profile and his distinctive competencies, not every possible strategic option will be likely to be successful. Based on the competitor's strengths, some future courses of action may be more likely to be pursued by the competitor than other options.

- *Where is the competitor vulnerable?* Given that a competitor cannot be strong on all items, it may be beneficial to identify weak spots that may serve as target for competitive strategic action.

- *How would competitive retaliations be stimulated?* In order to anticipate potential severe reactions to ones own strategic choices, it is useful to evaluate potential retaliations by competitive firms on alternative strategic courses of action.

The above questions can partly be answered by a careful analysis of the competitive landscape as described in the foregoing. A crucial factor in successfully conducting a competitor analysis is information. Although competitive intelligence is difficult, information on (potential) competitors may come from unexpected, close-by sources. In Box 3.3 we indicate some potentially useful information sources in order to obtain competitive information.

Box 3.3: Potential sources of information on competitors

Own observation
- desk research
- market research
- sales force
- product analysis/reverse engineering

Competitors on themselves
- annual reports
- advertisements
- press releases
- personnel advertisements
- former employees

Others on competitors
- customers
- industry experts
- financial analysts
- distributors
- other competitors
- the press/media
- market research agencies

3.4.5   ANALYSIS OF THE MACRO-ENVIRONMENT

Every industry is affected by developments in the macro-environment. In essence, all organizations are affected by the same developments, although the extent to which organizations successfully cope or take advantage of these developments differs substantially. Also, developments may potentially influence one industry more severely than another. For organizations it is important to identify or even anticipate macro-developments in order to evaluate their potential impact on the industry and the organization. Obviously, these developments may have a significant effect on strategic choices. Consider, for example, the impact of technological developments on firms. Financial service providers find themselves confronted with information technology developments that not only affect their operations in a significant way (back office), but that also have a (potentially) substantial effect on customer relations. Generally, six types of macro-developments are distinguished. These include technological, economic, demographic, legal/political, social-cultural and physical developments. Obviously, not all developments will deserve equal managerial attention at any point in time for each organization. In this respect, Ansoff suggests an approach known as *strategic environmental issue management.* In essence, for large organizations this entails a continuous scanning of the environment and identification of (potentially) relevant issues that arise from the developments that are observed. A classic example is *Shell*, an organization that continuously monitors the environment, especially with respect to technological and physical developments, on the basis of which they formulate scenarios of potential future environments in order to anticipate viable strategic options. As large companies will be affected by all kinds of macro-developments, a broadly focused environmental scanning may be necessary. Smaller organizations may choose to monitor selected types of developments within their environment, depending on their type of business. A major disadvantage of selective attention to macro-developments may be that the organization is myopic to developments that may pose a thread to their type of activity. Therefore, periodic attention for dynamics other than in one's industry may be fruitful. An instrument that can be used to identify potentially impactful developments and assess their affect on the organization is *cross-impact analysis*.

Cross-impact analysis

The central focus of cross-impact analysis is on assessing how macro-developments influence each other. Developments that occur simultaneously may enforce their effect on organizations. For any particular organization, it is important not only to assess potentially influential developments, but to identify such enforcing effects in order to anticipate them in an adequate way.

Procedure

A cross-impact analysis can be conducted in the following way. First, by means of environmental scanning (e.g. through desk research or sales force information) potentially important developments in the macro-environment are identified. In the event that developments refer to the same phenomenon, developments may be merged into one underlying trend. Second, based on supporting information (desk research, expert opinion etc.) the probability that the development will actually occur should be estimated for each development. Finally, an evaluation should be made of the extent to which the developments effect each other. This is best done in a two-dimensional matrix with the developments on both dimensions. An evaluation of each cross-impact can be done either in a qualitative or a quantitative way. A qualitative assessment may be given in terms such as "will have a critical influence on", "will severely affect", "will affect", "will have a minor effect" or "will have no or negligible effect". Quantitatively, evaluations may be given by assessing probabilities that one development will affect another. Delphi techniques (by obtaining expert opinions in several recurring rounds) may be used to make appropriate evaluations. This will result in an understanding of which developments will be most pervasive in their influence on other developments and to what extent developments jointly may have a substantial influence on the industry. This also marks the starting point of the fourth phase of the analysis, assessing the (cross-) impact of developments on the organization. To what extent will developments affect the organization's activities and opportunities and how will developments influence the firm's relative capability profile? As practice has shown, some developments may have a substantial effect on an industry and the critical success factors that are important in that industry.

3.5 PRACTICAL GUIDELINES FOR EXECUTION

Based on the external analysis, the organization should have obtained insight in opportunities and threats in its environment. Thus, opportunities for current or future customer value creation that are distinctive to competitive value creation are ideally identified. Also, potential discrepancies between value creation activities and value capture possibilities are assessed (for example, in case value created by the organization only results in enhanced profit margins for distributors rather than the organization itself, one may question the effectiveness of the value creation activity; of course, other potentially positive effects may be strived for, such as enhanced commitment from distributors). In conjunction with the distinctive resources and capabilities to be identified in the internal analysis (next chapter), the external analysis is an essential basis for (marketing) strategy formulation. Therefore, it is extremely important that an external analysis is executed in a profound way. We conclude this chapter on external analysis by providing some practical guidelines that may help to do so.

1. First of all, one has to realize that identification of opportunities for creating customer value requires sufficient understanding of both customers' needs and competitors' capabilities. In practice, strategic marketing plans are often found to suffer from relatively scarce attention to *really* understanding customer markets and competitive dynamics and competitors' motives and strategies. Rather, plans often take a descriptive approach by only "painting the picture of the industry", in stead of aiming to understand the (future) drivers in the industry. Moreover, a profound understanding of both customers (' behavior) and competitor profiles will help to formulate a comprehensive implementation plan.
2. External developments are more meaningful to interpret if their relevance is assessed in the light of the organization's own (distinctive) resources and capabilities. Although a structured and systematic confrontation of external developments and issues with organizational resources and capabilities is the focus of the SWOT-analysis, and therefore should not be part of the external analysis, an interpretation of external issues based on an organizational reference frame will help to distinguish between potentially more and less relevant environmental developments and issues.
3. The analyses within an external analysis should be supported by as much sources as possible. This will enhance the reliability of the analyses and, therefore, of the conclusions that are drawn based on them. Of course, this will also depend on the availability of sources and their reliability. In any event, the analysis should be supported by solid arguments and, if possible, quantitative justifications.
4. Ultimately, the external analysis results in a summary report expressed by opportunities for obtaining competitive advantage and threats that may erode or inhibit advantage. In order to enable convergence to those issues that (potentially) are most important to an organization, it is advisable to rank opportunities and

threats according to their relevance. A cross-impact analysis may help to do so. As a SWOT-analysis with an input of, say, 25 opportunities and threats will be difficult to execute, it is best to concentrate on, say, the top 5 opportunities and the top 5 threats in the first place. This will help to focus the analysis on the issues that seem to matter most.

5. Finally, it is tempting to conduct an external analysis based on information that is currently available to the organization or that is relatively easy accessible in the first place. This should be avoided at all times as this will result in a lack of attention to some aspects of the analysis and may stimulate a myopic view of the market and industry.

3.6 NOTES

[1] Bijmolt, Frambach and Verhallen (1996).
[2] Jain (1997).
[3] Kotler (2000).
[4] Porter (1985).
[5] Grove (1996).
[6] Weick (1979).
[7] Kotler (2000).
[8] See also Hooley, Saunders and Piercy (1998), p. 34-35.
[9] See e.g., Day (1994).
[10] Clancy and Shulman (1991).
[11] See e.g. Hutt and Speh (1995).
[12] Models that analyze consumer behavior include for example: Howard and Sheth (1969) and Engel, Blackwell and Miniard (1986); models that analyze industrial buyer behavior include: Webster and Wind (1972) and Choffray and Lilien (1980).
[13] Abell (1980).
[14] Source: Abell (1980)
[15] Day (1990).
[16] See e.g., Stern, El-Ansary and Coughlin (1996).
[17] See Kim and Mauborge (1997).
[18] Porter (1980).
[19] Coyne and Subramaniam (1996).
[20] Source: Porter (1980)
[21] Markides (1998), p. 32
[22] Hooley, Saunders and Piercy (1998).

CHAPTER 4

IDENTIFYING RESOURCES AND CAPABILITIES FOR VALUE CREATION: THE INTERNAL ANALYSIS

> '...the case for resource analysis rests not only upon the observation that contemporary developments in strategy have overemphasized external analysis... but also that resources are the fount from which the firm's profits flow'
>
> ---Robert M. Grant

4.1 INTRODUCTION

Considering a company as the vehicle for customer value creation we need to carefully analyze its strengths and weaknesses. This is what is normally referred to as the internal analysis. It concerns an appraisal of an organization's resources and capabilities in the context of value creation opportunities and other external developments. Resources are the organization's assets, knowledge and skills. Capabilities can be defined as the organization's ability to effectively make use of its resources.[1] In the past decade, the view that an organization's resources and capabilities are the drivers of an organization's strategic opportunities in the marketplace has received increasing support. This *Resource-Based View* of the firm argues that competitive advantage is to a large extent determined by the uniqueness of the organization's resources and capabilities. Roads to future advantage can be found by identifying unique opportunities to exploit these resources in current and new markets. This is different from the more traditional, contingency-based view that argues that organizations have to adapt to their (changing) environment (strategic 'fit'). Both views seem to complement each other, although dependent on the organization's objectives and its situation one may be more relevant than the other. In the event that an organization fails to systematically evaluate and identify its unique resources and the opportunities to exploit them, little leverage will be obtained from its stronghold in the marketplace. Such an organization is less likely to be among those that make a unique and/or creative contribution in the market. On the other hand, a company that does not systematically evaluate its organizational resources and capabilities against the key success factors of the market particularly when important changes occur (e.g., superior competitive supply, changing customer demand, introduction of superior technology etc.) face the danger of their competencies becoming obsolete. Thus, the ability to create superior customer value may require both an appraisal of the organizational resources and capabilities with respect to their exploitation opportunities (the resource-based appraisal) and an appraisal in the light of current and future market conditions (the market-based appraisal). It is the objective of the internal analysis to execute such an appraisal. As the effectiveness of the market-based appraisal is largely dependent on the organization's insight into the key success factors in the marketplace, we suggest conducting the internal analysis after the analysis of the organization's environment (the external analysis).

After briefly outlining the theory underlying the internal analysis, we will discuss instruments that can be used while conducting such an analysis. These instruments can and should be used in conjecture to each other. Only by using different instruments that focus either on different processes within the organization or that address the organization from different points of view, a comprehensive insight in the factors that enable or inhibit value creation by an organization will be obtained.

4.2 THEORETICAL BACKGROUND OF THE INTERNAL ANALYSIS
In order to operate successfully in the market a company must have resources and capabilities to create unique sustainable customer value, and thus to obtain, defend and sustain a competitive advantage in the market place. Resources and capabilities are sometimes referred to as *distinctive competencies* or *core competencies*. These latter concepts are often used interchangeably, but they are different. Core competencies are those competencies which form the heart of the company and which drive the value creation process and thus explain its current position.[2] Distinctive competencies are those things that a company is particularly good at doing *and* that they can do better than competitors. These are uniquely valued by customers and result in a true competitive advantage and thus a good market position. In a successful company, core competencies will coincide with distinctive competencies. Less successful companies' core competencies are no longer distinctive competencies because customers do not value them anymore or because they are no longer superior to or different from those of competitors.

The relationship between the two concepts and the organizational resources and capabilities, referred to as the organizational capacity to create and deliver superior customer value, is depicted in Figure 4.1.

Which elements pertain to the company's capacity to create and deliver superior customer value? In the first place one has to consider all the tangible and intangible assets that the organization has. These assets may exist within the company's functional areas or within its support services. Second, the relationships that exist between the various assets must also be included in the analysis. The company routines and systems that are formed by the organization to exploit its resources are an equally important part of the company's competencies as are the links with parties in the firm's direct

58

environment. Increasingly, firms use partnerships and/or customers to develop and produce product or service offerings. Thus, in addition to the organization's "internal resources", the analysis of resources and capabilities should include partnership-based and customer-based resources.[3] This is why it is only when the internal links and direct external relationships have been examined that the actual capacities of a company can be thoroughly understood. Therefore, it is better to talk about the *internal environment* of the company rather than its internal situation. The former is a more comprehensive term than the latter. Third, not only the company's current assets should be looked at. Potential assets and assets to which it has or can obtain access are also important. In fact these optional resources often hide surprising and promising opportunities for customer value creation.

Figure 4.1: Organizational capacity, core competencies, distinctive competencies and competitive advantage

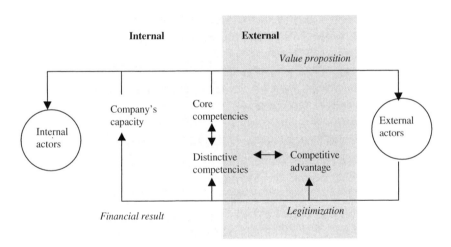

The goal that a company is striving for in deploying its assets is to create superior customer value. This will help to build and secure the company's competitive advantage in the market that will make it profitable in the long run. In essence, two main roads to value creation can be identified. [4] First, superior customer value can be created by means of differentiating the firm's offering. Differentiation can be accomplished in several ways, e.g. via the organization's product (innovation), marketing channel (e.g., on-line purchasing opportunities), communication (e.g., distinctively creative advertising for in essence undifferentiated products—a good example is *Absolut Vodka* that has created a distinctive campaign for a product that is homogenous by law), etc. Second, providing offerings that are similar to that of competitors but offered at a lower price create value. Lower cost levels will help achieve such a position. A structurally lower cost structure for serving customers may emerge from production efficiencies (e.g., using superior production technology), distribution efficiency and convenience (e.g., Michael Dell was able to lower distribution cost substantially through on-line sales of computers), and specific services (e.g., banks using self-service technology).

In order to evaluate to what extent an organization is capable of realizing a competitive advantage in the market place, its efforts need to be related to both the performance of competitors and the customers' appreciation for what the company does and the products it offers.[5] Criteria used for benchmarking against the company's competitors are for instance relative market share and relative profit levels. Criteria relating to the customers are customer satisfaction and loyalty. As far as the customers are concerned, it is important to note that they are less interested in the company's actual performance. The way in which the customer perceives and experiences the company's efforts is the most important thing. The bottom line is the extent to which customers value the organization's offering and whether they purchase it and remain loyal. It is essential to use both the competitive perspective and the customer perspective (the firm has to be both efficient and effective). However, depending on the type of industry and whether the company has (until now) been using costs as its main competitive weapon or whether it has been following a differentiation strategy, the perspective will tend to be either more competitor-oriented or customer-oriented. The seemingly less important of the two must never be neglected, though.

The competitive game in the market is not only about *creating* customer value and, thus, competitive advantage. Retaining the advantage is just as important. An advantage that erodes quickly is of far less value than a sustainable advantage. Erosion generally occurs through imitation or innovation: less successful or new providers copy the behavior of successful providers, or a provider may try to outdo a competitor by shifting to new and more effective or efficient technology (*leap-frogging*). As far as imitation is concerned, key elements are information about and access to sources of advantage. In order to be able to copy behavior, competitors must be aware that certain competencies, or combinations of competencies, are the decisive factor in achieving success. If this limiting condition is met, it still remains to be seen whether the competition will be able to acquire the knowledge concerned or gain access on competitive terms (cf. *mobility barriers* and *barriers of entry*). Highly successful companies distinguish themselves usually from less successful ones through their greater openness of information. The more successful ones concentrate on achieving competencies that are difficult to copy and they constantly innovate them. Less successful companies on the other hand, with few distinctive competencies, have a tendency to isolate themselves. They are –quite rightly—afraid to grant outsiders insight into the day to day running of their company because of their lack of distinctive competencies.

Having looked at the elements of the internal analysis and the relationships between internal capacities and how they contribute to the market position of the company, we can now draw the link between the internal analysis and potentially viable strategic options. Although a company will have to adapt to the external environment or at least will have to take into account the developments in its environment (*contingency theory*), it can also search and enter those markets that fits best the competencies it has (*strategic choice theory* and *resource based view theory*). In the (marketing) strategy literature this is also referred to as thinking *beyond fit*. It shows that the internal analysis is not simply a supplement to the external analysis but also essential in order to gain a complete picture of the company's real strategic options. Both the external environment and the internal resources could present valuable starting points for marketing strategy formulation and choices.

4.3 CONTENTS OF THE INTERNAL ANALYSIS

Above, we indicated that the objective of an internal analysis is twofold. First, the internal analysis aims to evaluate the opportunities that an organization has to exploit its current resources and capabilities in order to create future superior customer value. Second, the internal analysis needs to find out which new resources and capability requirements it is facing given the changes in key success factors and the emerging opportunities for new customer value creation identified in the external analysis.

Accordingly, we define an internal analysis as follows:

An internal analysis refers to the systematic evaluation of organizational resources and capabilities that are (potentially) available to the organization with the objective to obtain insight into the organization's current and future abilities to create and sustain a competitive advantage in the market by delivering superior customer value.

Hence, the internal analysis provides insight into the organizational capacity to create and deliver customer value that is superior to and distinctive from competing offerings. Each organizational resource and capability may be classified as either relative strong or relative weak when compared to (potential) competitors' profiles. First a general evaluation of the organization tends to be made discussing the competencies within their context and explaining the value judgement as weak or strong. Next, a summary list is made to provide a quick overview of the firm's resource situation. It will also help the evaluation against the important trends in the environment and thus future key success factors. Although these evaluations often tend to be rather subjective and full of management or employee's opinions[6], we plea for a more fundamental approach. The strengths-and-weaknesses should be based on a comprehensive analysis that includes an analysis of organizational assets, knowledge and skills. This includes the (internal and external) resources that are available or (potentially) accessible by the organization and its capability to make effective use of these resources in a distinctive way (sometimes referred to as its "business model").

In order to analyze the internal environment systematically, a structured analysis of the firm's value creation capacity should take place. We distinguish between three main elements that need to be considered.

- First, the organizational resources and capabilities in general need to be assessed. This includes organizational strengths and weaknesses with respect to the organization's primary business process, its supporting activities and its capabilities to link and make use of resources in an effective and distinctive way (relative to competition). This is referred to as the organizational audit. In essence, the organizational audit should identify the opportunities an organization (potentially) has in order to create superior customer value based on its (accessible) resources and capabilities.
- Second, a *marketing audit* is required. It relates both to the organization's current ways of delivering customer value and its potential (capacity) to do so otherwise. The marketing audit should cover all aspects of customer value delivery, such as customer service interactions, customer relationship management (CRM), customer information, the deployment of marketing instruments, and the organization of the marketing function and activities.
- Third, a financial audit should be conducted in order to obtain a detailed insight into the company's financial resources and performance. The company's financial performance should be evaluated using the industry average and average of its strategic group as a benchmark. Tracing the company performance over a period of 3-5 year makes it also possible to evaluate the volatility in performance and its ultimate increase or decrease. An analysis of the cost development and a breakdown of the operating results across the various departments and product lines may also help. Such analyses help to locate where (possible) problems occur. The firm's liquidity and solvency must also be examined in order to obtain insight into the organization's financial strength and flexibility.

We will now take a closer look at these three elements of the internal analysis by discussing strategic tools that can be deployed in each part. It is important to note that all three analyses (audits) together should provide the insight needed to satisfy the objectives of the internal analyses that were pointed out in the beginning of this paragraph.

4.4 STRATEGIC TOOLS

4.4.1 DEPLOYMENT OF INSTRUMENTS IN THE ORGANIZATIONAL AUDIT
We discuss three different strategic tools that may help evaluate the company's opportunities and qualities as a generator of future customer value.

First, we will discuss Michael Porter's concept of the *Value Chain*.[7] This concept identifies different primary and supportive (secondary) functions that should be evaluated upon their value adding contribution. The model is especially useful to analyze to what extent the organization currently utilizes primary and secondary activities to create value delivery opportunities and to what extent additional opportunities are possible. Porter distinguishes between value creation opportunities through differentiation or advantageous low cost positions. Differentiation may lead to customer value creation in the event that the organization is capable of providing an offer that is in one or more ways superior to competing offerings. Relative low cost positions may result in superior customer value delivery in the case that the organization offers comparable or even superior offerings to their customers at lower customer cost.

Second, we will discuss the *Activity System*, which is a more recently developed tool by Porter (1996). It can be used to analyze how organizational resources and activities are interrelated and create or fail to create "uniqueness". The system captures in essence the business model that is used by a particular organization, and as such, the degree to which relatively unique customer value is created and delivered. Finally we will discuss McKinsey's 7-S framework. It is used to analyze the content and cocktail of organization strategy, structure, systems and skill, staff, leadership style and superordinate goals. The model is especially useful for analyzing the degree of consistency within the organization's approach and to which the organization is receptive to change.

The Value Chain

In order to understand how a company gains a competitive advantage in the market, we need to further analyze the company as a set of activities. We must examine the many different activities that the company carries out in the field of design, production, marketing, delivery and promotion of its products. Each of these activities can contribute to the company's relative cost position and form or create a basis for differentiation. Based on this idea, a company can be seen as a *value chain* that creates added value for its customers in a unique way compared to its competitors. An essential point here is the notion that the value chain 'consists of' value activities and profit margin. Value activities are the physical and technological activities that the company conducts. They are the building blocks with which a company creates a product (or service) that is valuable to customers. The margin is the difference between the total value and the collective costs incurred in creating the product.

Within the concept of the company as value chain, a distinction is made between primary activities and support activities (see Figure 4.2). Primary activities are those activities that relate to both the creation of the product and its sale/ transfer to the customer as well as the after-sales service offered. Supporting activities support the primary activities and each other by taking care of general acquisition, technology, the management of human capital and the infrastructure of the company.

Figure 4.2: The Value Chain[8]

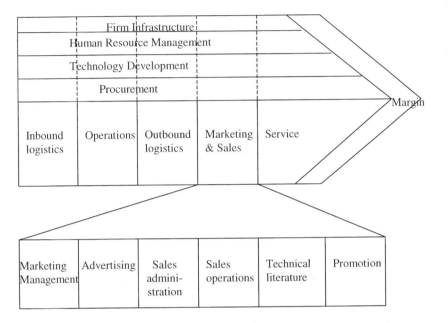

Although value chain activities are the building blocks of competitive advantage, and may be thought of as separate elements, they seldom exist in isolation. This is also why the value chain is presented as a collection of dependent activities, i.e. as a system. Consequently also the interrelationships or connections need to be analyzed. We need to understand the way in which the interdependencies contribute to more added value or hamper value creation. Linkages can refer to content-related co-ordination but may also include sequential co-ordination. Both paths can bring competitive advantage.

Within the value chain we must identify the *cost and uniqueness drivers*. These are the elements that either individually or in combination make a direct contribution to the costs of the firm's product offerings (i.e., the differentiation). Only then can we know how the company's competitive advantage is embedded in the organization, how it is constructed and how it develops.

In addition to internal *linkages*, the external links are essential. It is important to realize that the value chain of a company is linked with the value chains of suppliers, customers and so forth. Added value can also arise here. With many companies focusing on their core business and outsourcing several activities value linkages are more important than ever before. Also information and communication technology have their impact. Use of these technologies (often by cooperating) may help increase convenience for the customer and lower cost. The actual value of what the company produces is thus not only determined by the internal situation. The synergy between its own value chain and that of other organizations (competitors, customers, universities, research organizations etceteras) can make a unique contribution when creating customer value. Therefore, it is essential to obtain insight into these strategically significant external linkages and establish their influence on cost and differentiation.

The value chain may sometimes be difficult to apply. The easiest solution is concentrating on the concept's basic idea: to identify in which way and where the company creates its added value or achieves lower costs. First focusing on the main added value of the company helps to identify the main deficiencies also. In addition the following procedure can be used.

- Begin by identifying the company's primary and supporting activities. For this, we must first determine the point of departure. What type of company is it? For example, is it a commercial firm or a production company? Is a product or a service produced? Such specific basic principles shift the emphasis within the value chain.
- Next, we look for those activities that make up a relevant share of the costs. Then look for the elements that help the firm's (product) differentiation.
- Then we look at the *linkages*. We distinguish five categories that all need our attention and should be evaluated:
  - linkages between primary activities;
  - linkages between primary and supporting activities;
  - linkages with the value chain of supplier firms;
  - linkages with the value chain of customers;
  - linkages with the value chain of other market parties.
- Based on the above we can identify potential areas of improvement. This may relate either to individual activities or to (internal and external) linkages. It is important not to adhere too strictly to the way in which activities are defined at present. In fact, rearranging and redefining activities has a better chance of resulting in the identification of new forms of customer value creation, and thus finding new sources of advantage. In other words, look for possible innovations in *cost* and *uniqueness drivers*.
- Draw a general conclusion on the shape the organization is in. Include the (internal/external) opportunities to go over the value chain analysis once more. Finally, repeat the previous steps using a true outward-looking-in perspective. It will bring a fresh new way of looking at things and may light new ideas for value creation.

The Activity System

Another instrument that helps to provide a clearer understanding of the cohesiveness of activities is the *Activity System*.[9] As in the value chain analysis, the idea underlying this model is that the differentiating (unique) position of an organization comes from the range of resources, skills and/or activities present and their level of cohesiveness. Whereas the *Value Chain analysis* is a structured analysis of the various activities in the primary industrial process and its supporting processes, in the *Activity System* the emphasis is on revealing the full range of activities that determines its strategic position. This can be an important combination of activities and resources as the example of the *Southwest Airlines* activity system shown in Box 4.1 illustrates.[10]

Box 4.1: Example—The Southwest Airlines Activity System[11]

An activity system is useful for analyzing and strengthening an organization's strategic cohesiveness. A number of questions can guide this process and as such help the company's internal analysis and implementation phase. First one should consider whether each activity is consistent with the organization's overall positioning (in the form of the variety offered, the needs met, and the types of client who are reached). Those who are responsible for each activity should indicate how other activities within the organization improve or hamper the activity they are responsible for. Second one should look for ways to reinforce the system by investigating how the interactions between the activities can create additional synergies. Finally, can changes in one activity make other activities redundant?

The darker colored elements form the heart of the strategic position and are implemented by means of clusters of activities which are strongly inter-linked (and which are shown in a lighter color). The Southwest Airlines activity system shows that this company's unique strategic position is based on supplying a 'lean' transport service at a highly competitive price. The resources, activities and market strategy are tailored in a very consistent way and create synergy. Because there is a particular group of customers in the market that relates to this type of customer value the uniqueness compared to other providers is recognized making the company a financial success.

The 7-S framework

McKinsey's 7-S framework is a useful instrument for gaining insight into the organization's general situation and the degree to which the organization is receptive to and capable of changing or reinventing itself. The model comprises seven important elements, which individually and in combination constitute an organization. The model contains both hard and soft variables. A priori, however, it is not clear what the weight and/or the relevance of each element is. The model is shown in Figure 4.3 and will be discussed in detail next.

Figure 4.3: The 7-S Framework[12]

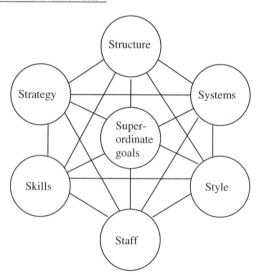

Strategy

Strategy refers to the actions, which are intended, either anticipating or in response to developments in the external environment. The method of formulating strategy, the quality of the strategy content and the method of implementation may be involved in the perspective.

Structure

Structure is the way in which the organization is divided into smaller units together with the links between them (established relationships, balance of power and behavioral norms).

Superordinate goals

The objectives of the company indicate what it is aiming at and what sort of aspirations it has. These objectives may be written down but this is not essential. They may be known only to the management or generally known within the organization. If the latter is the case then they have a clear function in the sense that they give direction to the organization ('we all have the same aims'). Superordinate goals are thus literally the fundamental ideas around which a company has been and is being built.

Systems

Systems comprise all the formal and informal procedures and processes according to which the organization works. Examples include budget systems, training systems, administration systems and management information systems. Systems form a highly integral part of the organization because they are the mechanisms according to which the day-to-day routines take place.

Style

Style has to do with leadership behavior and the culture of the organization. It is particularly important to look at whether the leadership style corresponds to the type of organization and the environment in which the company operates. Moreover, 'the way we do things around here' is an important gauge of the degree to which the company is open to new things.

Staff

Staff pertains to the personnel in a broad sense. People are an important company 'asset' and require considerable attention. Good personnel management is therefore essential. Matters such as average age, years of service, absenteeism, turnover, average level of training etc. are important indicators of whether adequate attention is being devoted to this variable.

Skills

Skills refers to the knowledge and expertise possessed by the staff. The question is how well this is developed for each functional area. We have to check whether the company has 'state of the art' capabilities and knowledge or whether it is lagging behind or is missing skills in certain important areas.

It is important to note that the position of each of the 7-S's in Figure 4.5 is arbitrary. The strength and character of an organization is captured by the unique combination in the model. Still, when analyzing the organization simply filling in the

S's is a good starting point. Next the links between the different elements should be assessed. Some suggestions for use are:

- First identify the company's main assets per S or area. Start with those things that come up when simply looking at the organization and characterize them. Next add a value judgement clarifying the benchmark used (e.g. main competitor or industry average). In addition, interview managers and listen to the stories told by other employees. . The topics that come up can be classified within the 7 S model. It is a good idea to subdivide some of the S's. For example, the S for skills can be broken down into its various functional areas; 'Style' can include both the firm's main culture but also subcultures. 'Strategy' may relate not only to the general strategy, but also to the functional strategies.

- For each S we can draw on theory. In this way it is possible to further define or analyze the structure, the strategy and the leadership style. Aids such as Mintzberg's organization models[13], Porter's generic strategy types[14] and Blake and Mouton's leadership styles[15] can be used. Falling back on these more specific concepts also makes the analysis more convincing.

- The application of the 7-S model result in a real analysis of the organization. It should not merely be a description of the existing situation. To prevent the latter, focus among other things on the following questions:

- What are the good and bad points about the organization, given the (future) critical success factors that have emerged from the external analysis?

- What positive and negative elements distinguish us from our competitors?

- What do our clients and we consider to be our strong points?
  Box 4.2 presents some questions that may be helpful in applying the 7-S Framework.

- In addition to creating insight into the development of each S and the way in which this relates to the competition (reference point), the balance between the S's and the relationships between them must also be analyzed. Are they consistent? Are strategy, skills, structure, and leadership style tailored to each other?

Box 4.2: Guiding questions for applying the 7-S framework

Skills/staff/style

- How effectively do the separate functional areas (including R&D) perform?
- How effectively do the support services function?
- How effectively are the line and staff roles performed?
- How effectively does the top management perform?
- How effectively does the middle management perform?
- How effectively does the operational staff perform?
- Education and training level
- Culture (product-driven, sales-driven, customer-driven)
- Degree to which the organization is open to change

Structure/systems

- How efficient are the means of production and how well does the primary production process function (efficiency/effectiveness)?
- How effectively does the logistics system function?
- How good is the administrative system; the management information?
- How good are the support resources and the functioning of the support processes (staff recruitment, automation, budgeting, etc.)?
- How highly developed is the organization's flexibility (structure, culture)?
- How sound is the financial situation (trends in costs, profit/profitability trends, profit contribution to departments/product lines)?

Strategy/superordinate goals

- Is there an effective mission statement?
- How well does our strategy work (pay off)?
- What is the form/content/functioning of strategy-formulation?
- Are the objectives realistic yet at the same time sufficiently challenging?

Co-ordination

- Is the strategy tailored to the environment?
- Is the structure tailored to the strategy?
- Are the systems tailored to the size of the company?
- Are the systems tailored to the strategy?
- Is the structure tailored to the size of the company?
- Is the leadership style tailored to the strategy?
- Are the skills tailored to the strategy?
- Are the skills tailored to the systems?
- Is the company culture tailored to the strategy?

Note: The elements/questions listed are intended as a starting point for analysis; the list is not exhaustive.

4.4.2 FINANCIAL AUDIT

Often marketers eschew financial analyses. However, an analysis of the company's financial situation should be part of any decent strategic plan just like clear budgets and financial targets should be part of any annual marketing plan. Below we will focus on indicators for understanding the firm's basic financial position, cost structure and room for investments.

Content of the financial audit

The significance of the financial analysis goes deeper than simply analyzing the company's existing and potential (financial) resources. We are interested in the *commercial position* of the company in a broad sense (its ability to finance certain strategies and marketing programs). Is the company financially sound and is its continuity assured? This question should also be addressed relative to benchmarks such as the firm's main competitors and the industry's average.

Three matters are of essential importance in monitoring the financial situation:
- the profitability of the activities (and, related, shareholders value);
- the development in costs and returns (including the cash flow balance);
- the company's short and long term financing structure and viability.

From a strategic perspective the most important indicator is profitability (shareholder value). The financial results achieved by the company are an indicator for the 'overall' quality of the strategy it pursues. Many companies include financial targets in their business objectives. These include, for example, a minimum net profit level, Return On Investment, Return On Assets, or a certain growth in turnover. Whether these objectives are reached or not says something about the success of the strategy. It is also important, however, to relate the values to internal criteria. Taking a look at the company's history and the market situation can be of use here. It gives an idea of how feasible and/or realistic the objectives and the management ambitions are. In particular, the trend in profitability must be examined. The second important area from a strategic perspective concerns the costs and returns. A detailed picture of the development in the pattern of costs and returns provides an insight into the efficiency of the company. What are the most important cost-creating activities (cf. Value Chain)? What are the trends in the costs? If the costs are growing more rapidly than the turnover this may indicate a problem. An aspect that we can include in the analysis here is balancing the cash flows. Is a good balance achieved between the company's various activities, or is there a risk of unbalanced growth (compare also with the portfolio analysis). Third, with respect to the continuity of the company it is important to know whether the company can and will be able to meet its short-term and long-term financial commitments. This brings us to the company's liquidity and solvency. The financing structure of the company, however, is also relevant in connection with the potential for attracting liabilities. The available scope for investment is determined not only by the existing relationship between Equity and Liabilities but also by the current profitability. After all, a solid profitability reinforces the loan providers' impression that the company will be able to pay interest on the credit provided. In addition, current profitability provides the opportunity to reserve undistributed profits.

Instruments for financial auditing

Financial indicators, the Dupont-analysis and the product/SBU (Strategic Business Unit) portfolios are presented here as instruments. Since portfolios have a broader scope they are dealt with in the following section (marketing audit).

Easy tools for gaining an initial insight into a company's financial situation are financial indicators. One of the most important questions here concerns the correct guideline for assessment. Although general guidelines exist norms may vary widely between industries. Moreover, it is never sufficient to use a single indicator or looking at a single year. A good insight into the financial situation of a company can only be obtained by compiling a list of the figures covering a number of years so that their stability and trends can be analyzed. Box 4.3 shows a number of important indicators. They can form a useful starting point. As a supplement to these global indicators of the profitability analysis, an indicator for sales turnover has been included. If a particular turnover can be achieved with less capital without affecting the profit margin on the turnover, the profitability of the capital is increased. The capital is then better utilized.

Box 4.3: Financial indicators

Indicator:	Formula:	General guideline:
Solvency	Equity/Total Balance	0.6
Liquidity		
current ratio	Floating Assets/FE_{short}	1.5/2
quick ratio	Floating Assets -/- stocks/FE_{short}	1
Profitability		
Gross PTE	(Profit$_{before\ tax}$ + Interest on FE) / TE	
Gross PE	Profit$_{before\ tax}$ / E	
Net PE	Profit$_{after\ tax}$ / E	
Gross PFE	Interest on FE / FE	
*Rate of turnover**	Activity Costs / Total Balance	
Gross working capital	Sum of Floating Assets	
Net working capital	Gross working capital - total debts$_{short\ term}$	>0
Cash flow	Profit$_{after\ tax}$ + Depreciation (or: incomings - outgoings)	>0

* Can be calculated e.g., for: material stocks, stock of work in progress, stock of finished product and receivable accounts.

The Dupont-analysis or Dupont-diagram provides a method for examining the company's financial situation in a more comprehensive way (see Figure 4.4). It concerns a profitability analysis, stressing that the profitability over the Total Equity is a product of the Profit (before interest and as a percentage of the Turnover), and the Turnover Rate of the Total Equity.

In order to examine the developments in the costs and returns we need to break them down according to place of origin. We need to pay particular attention to significant entries/items, items which are rising fast(er) (than the turnover) and profit items which are falling.

Figure 4.4: The Dupont diagram

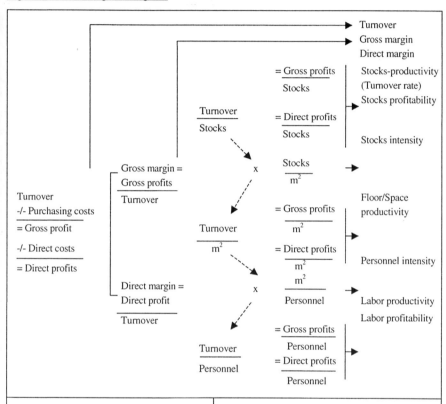

Gross profit/turnover = gross margin Turnover-stocks = stocks productivity or sales turnover Multiplying the gross margin with the rate of turnover gives the stocks profitability on the basis of gross profit or gross profit/stocks	By analogy, the floor/space and labor productivity can be calculated based on gross profits. The intensity criteria can be used to work out the floor/space productivity from the rate of turnover. Rate of turnover x stocks intensity = floor/space productivity. By analogy, labor productivity can be worked out by multiplying space productivity with personnel intensity

4.4.3 MARKETING AUDIT

Content of the marketing audit

The objective of a marketing audit is to evaluate the current processes of value delivery by an organization as well as its resources and capabilities to do so effectively, efficiently, and distinctively. As such, the marketing audit addresses all processes within the value chain that are involved in actually delivering the customer value created by the firm to the customer. In doing so, the marketing audit examines the effectiveness and efficiency of the company's marketing resources, capabilities and activities. In other words, the analysis needs to evaluate the marketing function and must indicate areas of improvement. It will show to what extent the current marketing function is suited to meet the requirements set by the environment, in particular its customers and competitors. Here, it is important to distinguish between the marketing function and the marketing department. In some organizations departments such as Research and Development or Sales (account management) carry out the marketing function. One should thus look beyond the marketing department. Central in the marketing audit should be the evaluation of marketing resources, capabilities, and activities, whether carried out by a specific marketing department, or other departments or people in the organization (e.g. top management).

With respect to the marketing function and the marketing program, various aspects need to be addressed in a marketing audit. These comprise the marketing strategy decisions (the *content* of the strategy), the tactical and operational marketing decisions (the *marketing mix*), and the organizational implementation of the marketing function (the *implementation* of the *marketing task*). An appraisal of the quality of the various aspects is essential in order to produce a genuine analysis and not just a description of the existing situation. A schematic guideline for carrying out a marketing audit will be discussed next.

Instrument for marketing auditing
Content of the strategy

In order to analyze the way in which the company has made its functional marketing decisions, and to see how this has evolved, the following aspects should be evaluated:
- segmentation (customer analysis, value identification, choice models, mapping);
- company positioning (value definition [per segment], brand strategy);
- portfolio situation;
- marketing objectives (share of the market, sales growth, customer satisfaction);
- performance:
    - Competition-oriented (portfolio/ MABA);
    - Customer-oriented (customer satisfaction, customer loyalty, sales distribution).

The marketing mix

In order to analyze the operational marketing decisions made by the firm, and to see how they have evolved, the marketing-mix should be evaluated. This may either relate to the traditional "4 P's" (Product, Place [distribution], Price and Promotion), or to the 7 "P's" for service (oriented) firms (plus: Process, Physical Evidence, Personnel). See Chapter 7 for specifics on each of the four "P's". The emphasis of the analysis will shift or other elements will be incorporated depending on the specific company situation. With respect to each marketing mix in.. .rument, the instrument objectives, strategy, activities and performance should be subject to evaluation. Thus, the effectiveness of all relevant marketing activities is systematically analyzed.

Implementation of the marketing function

In evaluating the company's marketing organization that is responsible for implementation of the marketing function, the items that were considered in the general organization audit can again be used. However, it is also a good idea to look at frequently recurring marketing weaknesses within the analysis process (see Box 4.4). Other general areas of attention within the analysis of the marketing organization include:

- Marketing organization (structure, number of staff, knowledge, management/ control instruments);
- Market research;
- Sales;
- Marketing information system (quality, conversion rate leads/ offers);
- Marketing as mentality within the organization;
- Method of evaluating marketing programs.

Box 4.4: Frequently recurring marketing weaknesses[16]

1.	Insufficient customer definition for product/ market analysis
2.	Lack of adequate knowledge of purchasing criteria/behavior of the customer/distributor for product/market analysis
3.	Too much emphasis on selling current products/ short term problems
4.	Lack of quantitative objectives
5.	Lack of top management involvement in product development
6.	Too little co-ordination between R&D, marketing and production in product development
7.	Too little co-ordination between marketing and sales
8.	Unclear service policy
9.	Overlapping distribution channels
10.	Lack of brand strategy

4.4.4 PORTFOLIOS

A *portfolio* is an instrument used in selecting optimal combinations of strategies for individual Strategic Business Units (SBU's) or product groups from a spectrum of options –based on an appraisal of the market attractiveness and the relative market position of the firm—taking account of the company's resource limitations.

In order to develop a portfolio, both the market attractiveness and the company's relative market position for each activity (SBU's or product groups) should be assessed. The particular strength of the portfolio is that it enables several SBUs or product groups to be studied and evaluated *at the same time*. This is the difference between the portfolio and the SWOT analysis. Whereas the SWOT analysis only provides a general insight into the `fit' between the company and its environment, the portfolio, by looking at several SBU's/ product groups at the same time, raises the question of whether the company has a balanced cash flow or not. A balanced cash flow is important in connection with the vitality and/or continuity of the enterprise. After all, it determines whether sufficient cash is being generated to make (essential) investments for the future. In addition, a portfolio picture provides a basis for a dynamic analysis of the relative company situation. The portfolio encourages the company to think in terms of its own actions as well as the competitors' reactions. Allocation decisions can be taken on the basis of it.

There are various types of portfolios available. First there are the portfolios whose axes consist of simple or single variables. The best known of these is the *Boston Consultancy Group* Matrix (*BCG*). It plots relative market share (relative to the company's main competitor or the market leader) against market growth. There is one important reservation regarding models of this type. Their design is generally so simple that they frequently fail to approximate the complexity of the market. This can lead to serious mistakes. Multi-factor models aim to meet this shortcoming to some extent. Examples of these include the *Shell* matrix and the *General Electric* matrix (cf. *Market Attractiveness, Business position Assessment* [MABA] analysis). These models are more generally applicable because a number of elements per axis are taken into consideration. Introducing other elements and weights for each axis, however, (as well as different scores for each activity) can still lead to different outcomes.

In addition to reservations relating to assumptions and scores, the way in which the market is defined also plays an important role in the correct handling of portfolios (e.g. the market for cars versus the market for sports cars). Moreover, a portfolio model assumes that the activities introduced within it are independent of each other although this is not necessarily always the case. Disinvesting in a particular activity or turning it into a money-spinner can have repercussions on the return from another activity. Running parallel to this is the criticism that many portfolios suggest standard strategies depending on the activity's position in the portfolio. This may lead to lost opportunities, since following the standard instructions leads to a self-fulfilling prophecy.

The execution of an MABA-analysis involves the following steps:
1.   Determine the level of analysis, including which activities will be incorporated into the portfolio picture (identification of SBU's or product clusters, etc.).
2.   Determine the relevant factors for Market Attractiveness (including market factors [e.g. size and growth], competition factors, financial-economic factors, technological factors and sociopolitical factors) and Business position Assessment (including (relative) market share, growth percentage, company size, margins/ profitability, negotiating position, people/resources and quality).
3.   Weigh the factors based on their relative importance. Make sure that the total weighting over the MA and BA factor adds up to 100 (or to 1).
4.   Determine the scores of each per element. Use for instance pluses and minuses (- -, -, 0, +, ++).
5.   Work out the total scores for the MA-axis and BA-axis for each firm activity.
6.   Draw the portfolio picture (see Figure 4.5).

Figure 4.5: MABA-portfolio

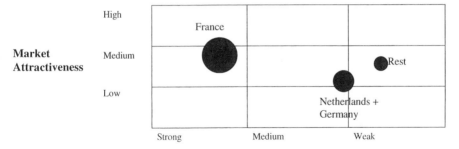

7.   Fill in activity circles, making sure they are the right size (representing the sales volume of the particular activity) and in the right place.
8.   Form an opinion:
      - examine the historical movement of the activities in the portfolio;
      - examine the distribution of activities across the portfolio and/or the cash flows.
9.   Consider strategic options:
      - the trends within the portfolio can be examined under consistent policy conditions;
      - alternative options for investment can be considered (including new activities which currently fall outside the portfolio).

In short, portfolios are powerful instruments. They deliver insights into the company's relative situation on the market. A portfolio can be used to look at how the company activities are spread as well as for evaluating the company's viability. A portfolio is also helpful for taking allocation and investment decisions. However, portfolio analyses have a special and somewhat difficult position in marketing reports using an external followed by internal analysis structure, as portfolios tend to combine aspects of both analyses. The two axes of the portfolio show not only elements of market attractiveness but also elements that reflect the company's relative position. One axis tends to relate more to the external analysis while the other axis is clearly embedded in the internal analysis. The definitive place, which we assign to the portfolio, depends on the question it is being used to answer. If it is being used to map the spread of current activities as well as for an 'assessment' of the company's continuity, then we place it internally. If it is more concerned with exploring alternative allocations and investment decisions, then one of the options is to place it externally. The most obvious place remains the internal analysis, however, assuming that the external analysis has already been addressed.

4.5 PRACTICAL GUIDELINES FOR EXECUTION

The outcome of the internal analysis should be an in-depth insight into the organization's distinctive competencies (strengths) and its weaknesses. Knowledge of the organization's current position and its potential for change is an essential starting point for evaluating optional future actions. Below, we indicated some points that should be taken into account in executing an internal analysis:

1. Given the strategic problem that was initially identified, it is important to determine the correct level for the internal analysis. An organization generally consists of more than one layer and it is usually possible to distinguish a company level, *strategic business units* and an operational level. The level at which the problem is relevant should form the point of departure for the internal analysis. Account must be taken, however, of potential synergetic links/ effects between departments and product lines. Otherwise we run the risk of `throwing the baby out with the bath water'. Genuine strategic problems relate to the enterprise level and/ or business unit level.

2. As a rule, it is not difficult for a group of managers to draw up a long list of their company's strong and weak points. But this should not be just a random list of elements. First, every area should be scrutinized. Second, the emphasis should lie on those elements that are really relevant, i.e. the critical success factors for the sector.

3. In strategy building, we are interested not only in the existing critical success factors but even more importantly in the future ones. In light of this we need to look not only at the company's actual competencies but to give equal consideration to its potential capacities/ competencies. To what extent is the company able to anticipate trends in the environment before competitors notice and can react? In which directions can the company expand, develop or recycle its capacities?

4. Sometimes an organization is hardly aware if at all of its actual distinctive competencies. A broad and deep perspective is therefore vital. Utilizing various points of view (from the competitors, customers, trade, etc.) can contribute to a better grasp and understanding of the company's actual situation and its actual competencies. With regard to the things which the enterprise does best, a distinction must be made between what the customers value and what they do not.

5. It is essential to be clear regarding the *reference point* that is used to determine whether the organization is good or bad at something. Is the company good at something compared with its own historical performance, the sector average or the most important competitor? Being in a strong position in comparison to the most important competitor says more than merely observing that the company has improved on its own performance in the previous year.

6. What is often missing in an internal analysis is an *interpretation*. Without this, the internal analysis tends to be a description rather than an analysis. As such it is of little use, as it does not draw any conclusions. This can usually be traced back to two causes: the way of appraisal and politics. Many managers tend to appraise things in a neutral way instead of specifically defining them as strong or weak. There are mainly political and business-cultural reasons for strong points being exaggerated and weak points being downplayed or vice versa![17] Calling in a consultant and/or asking for advice from an outside expert may help.

7. In the framework of constructing the internal analysis, it is best to incorporate one's own value judgement into each element but to leave any mention of the strengths and weaknesses of the organization until the final detailed analysis.

4.6 NOTES

[1] Day (1994).

[2] Prahalad and Hamel (1990).

[3] See also Adcock (2000), p. 36.

[4] See Porter (1980) and Day and Wensley (1988). A recent meta-analysis by Campbell-Hunt (2000) shows that cost and differentiation do act as high-level discriminators of competitive strategy designs.

[5] See Day and Wensley (1988).

[6] See e.g., Holbrook (1998).

[7] Porter (1985).

[8] Source: Porter (1985).

[9] Porter (1996).

[10] Source: Porter (1996), p. 73.

[11] Porter (1996).

[12] Source: Peters and Waterman (1982).

[13] Mintzberg (1983).

[14] Porter (1980).

[15] Blake and Mouton (1964).

[16] Adapted from: Jain (1997).

[17] Van der Lee (1991), p. 45.

CHAPTER 5

TOWARDS STRATEGIC ISSUES:
THE SWOT(I)-ANALYSIS

> *'SWOT...stands for strengths, weaknesses, opportunities and threats...the idea is to undertake a more structured analysis so as to yield findings which can contribute to the formulation of strategy. Although what follows is somewhat crude as an analytical device it has proved in practical application to be a helpful means of achieving these aims'.*
>
> ---Gerry Johnson and Kevin Scholes
> *Exploring Corporate Strategy*

5.1 INTRODUCTION

In the previous chapters we analyzed the external and then the internal environment of the company to identify opportunities and analyze the company's abilities for value creation. The external analysis helped to identify the key success factors for competing successfully, but also provided us with an understanding of future opportunities and the threats eroding current success factors. The internal analysis helped us to understand the company's strengths and weaknesses for value creation. The benchmark was the leading direct competitors or leaders of other industries. Operational aspects and underlying competencies were distinguished, and the firm's financial situation analyzed.

Although interesting, the real strategic value is only revealed when the results from the internal and external analyses are combined. Consistent with our definition of strategy, we need to look for the matches and mis-matches between the company and its changing environment. Management should identify most salient matches and mis-matches. These are the strategic issues that management needs to allocate its time and attention to trying to understand how the company's competencies fit the future key success factors of the industry. A somewhat dated but useful tool to help us is the SWOT analysis.

One of the oldest formulations in strategy is known by the acronym SWOT. It stands for Strengths, Weaknesses, Opportunities, and Threats. It concerns a simple diagnostic tool that entails the evaluation of the most important internal factors of an organization, i.e. its strengths and weaknesses, relative to the opportunities and threats in the organization's environment for identifying potential strategies. The analysis seems as well-known and important to strategy today as it was when it was first introduced decades ago.[1] Its simplicity has, without a doubt, contributed to this success. However, the joint analysis of strengths, weaknesses, opportunities and threats, is not an easy one. The labeling of trends as opportunities and threats is arbitrary or subjective at the least. Moreover there is no full proof method for identifying all opportunities and threats. Also identifying strengths and weaknesses often subjective due to a lack of clarification of the benchmark used. Given these experiences the recent voiced doubts about the tool's effectiveness should not come as a surprise. Survey research from Hill and Westbrook (1997) based on a sample of 50 British companies shows that many applications are characterized by long lists of non-discriminating items and that hardly anything is done with the conclusions coming from the analysis.[2] Table 5.1 summarizes the negative points associated with the analysis. Based on these results the authors conclude that SWOT is outdated and in need of a serious product recall. Abandoning it all together may even be the best option.

Several years earlier George Day (1990) identified similar problems of the tool. However, unlike Hill and Westbrook, he did not completely abandon the tool.[3] The question is why?

Table 5.1: Problems related to the SWOT-analysis[4]

- Long lists of items
- No priorities for items
- Unclear labeling or wording of items
- Lack of empirical evidence to prove items
- No link between the results of the SWOT analysis and the rest of the planning process

---

The main reasons would seem to be that SWOT is a methodologically sound approach for identifying strategic issues. It looks explicitly at the interface between the company and its environment and can thus be used to effectively identify fits and mis-fits between the two. The problems with the SWOT analysis stem mainly from the lack of objective market and company information and sloppy analyses by the people using the instrument. Or as Grant puts it: "Simplistic analyses …such as the ….SWOT analysis,… have given way to less-mechanistic analyses with sounder conceptual and empirical bases. …Yet, despite rapid development of the tools of strategy analysis, the gulf between strategic problems and managers' ability to find solutions to them remains as broad as ever".[5] Other reasons, next to garbage in-garbage out, for the SWOT's failing include the limited description and guidelines provided in most strategy books and the use of the SWOT analyses as a political tool in practice.

Understanding the tools strengths and weaknesses we suggest to keep the SWOT, but in a slightly modified form. We propose using it to match the core competencies of a company with the trends in its environment that represent opportunities to customer value creation and eroding forces of current value and underlying competencies. In our point of view the traditional "strengths and weaknesses" thus are no simple and long lists of superficial items but should involve carefully identified core competencies that lead or can lead to customer value for current or future customers. Similarly, the opportunities in the environment, identified in the external analysis, are no simple trends but current and future key success factors and/or threats that erode current sellers' competencies.

The theory behind the SWOT(I) analysis will be presented next in this Chapter. We will elaborate on the tool's content and also provide practical guidelines for successful use of the instrument.

5.2 THEORETICAL BACKGROUND OF THE SWOT(I) ANALYSIS

The objective of a strategic analysis is to systematically analyze a company's competence profile relative to the fundamental trends and shifts in the environment affecting key success factors. The result will help to effectively make the decisions regarding the company's future market strategy. A popular and simple tool for this is the SWOT analysis. It consists of an external and internal analysis followed by a confrontation of their results. The latter is generally done using a matrix. The external and internal analyses are used to identify opportunities/threats in the industry and strengths/weaknesses of the company, respectively. The confrontation serves to link the two outcomes and identify strategic issues. Strategic issues are salient interactions between the two dimensions. The instrument thus helps to narrow down the strategic problems. Management should focus its attention on the issues identified. They entail the potential matches and mis-matches between a company's core competencies and the (future) key success factors in the market place. Here lies the key for keeping current core competencies distinctive and for finding future competitive advantage.[6]

To understand the usefulness of SWOT we should look at its core ideas. Two key constructs come to mind, i.e. organization's distinctive competencies and organizations' competitive advantage. These are concepts that have attracted a lot of attention in the management literature and that have been linked recently. Competitive advantage refers to the superior position a company realizes in the market place. It is derived from unique customer value provided by a firm to its customers. This value can stem from lower cost or better product/service performance from the customer's point of view. A higher competitive advantage will lead to higher market share and higher Return on Investment for the supplier. When truly unique the advantage will be rooted in the company's competencies and competence structure and will be hard to imitate. Thus distinctive competencies are unique combinations of knowledge, capabilities and resources etc. However, "direct" resources are not the only sources of competitive advantage. "Indirect" resources, such as access to other firms' resources via partnerships also represent roads to advantage.

Looking for a relationship between the above-introduced concepts with the external and internal analyses, the conclusion is that opportunities/threats are closely related to competitive advantage. Strengths and weaknesses refer to the distinctive competencies. When a fit exists between a firm's competencies and the trends in the market place, i.e. opportunities and threats, its position will grow stronger. When the trends work erode the firm's position its competencies will become less unique and thus less distinctive.

5.3 INPUT FOR THE SWOT(I) ANALYSIS

The outcomes of the external and internal analyses are the input for the SWOT(I) analysis. Because many of the problems with the analysis stem from poor input we comment briefly on the input and make suggestions to ensure a certain level of quality.

5.3.1. EXTERNAL ANALYSIS

Managers generally find it easy to list opportunities and threats for their companies. However, not the length but the quality of the list is important. Here are some guidelines:

1. A sound external analysis should not only identify important trends, but also distill those trends that have a *significant impact* on the industry and market. Thus the influence of the trends needs to be demonstrated. The level of impact can be used to limit the number of trends. In stead of commenting that some competitors have a better performance find out why this is the case? Furthermore, regarding general trends, show the effect on the industry. When no effect is present omitting the trend from further analyses. Finally, turn opportunities and threats into key success factors. Characteristics of a key success factor is that it refers to unique knowledge, abilities, access and/or assets facilitating or hindering the building up of a competitive position, i.e. competitive advantage, in the market place in general or for servicing a specific market segment in particular. Key success factors are thus defined outside-in.

2. A checklist is a good and simple starting point for an external analysis (see Figure 5.1). However, it is no guarantee for not missing some important trends or aspects that can affect key success factors. To prevent this from happening two things must be considered. First, future rather than current key success factors need to be identified and analyzed. Second, using an iterative mode the internal analysis can be used to uncover important external factors. (Why have we identified certain strengths? Why are they important in our market and which trends regarding this aspect are taking place?)

3. Data need to be provided to support the interpretation of trends, their impact and timing. Objective data are to be preferred over subjective data or observations. In the

84

external analysis, a manager should not go by the data available but carefully determine the information need and try to obtain it. Only when data are really unobtainable we may resort to estimates.

Figure 5.1: Schema for input for the SWOT(I) Analysis[7]

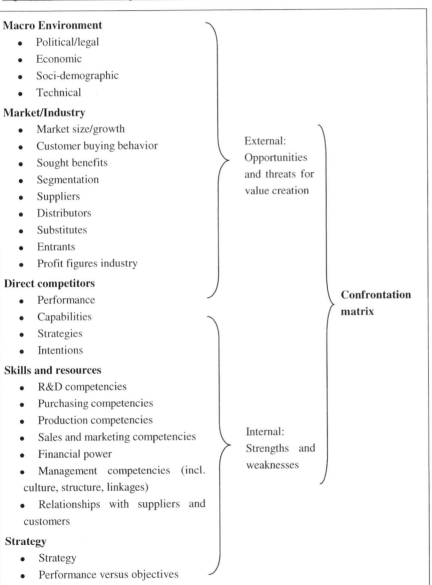

4. Because a strategic plan is about future business and strategy using extrapolating past trends or making forecasts based on last years market figures is unacceptable. A sound external analysis will show the market dynamics and particularly focus on identifying future trends. Furthermore data should be presented in a systematic and accessible order facilitating their interpretation (e.g. year to year percentages and forecasts).

5.3.2 INTERNAL ANALYSIS

Also for an internal analysis meaningless lists of strong and weak points should be omitted. Note the following:

1. Due to company politics little discriminating value is often to be found in the listing of the company's strengths en weaknesses. To prevent this from happening managers should clarify their point of reference. The best benchmark is the company's main or strongest competitor.

2. The internal analysis should not focus on general competencies but on specific ones, particularly those that are clearly linked to delivering of superior customer value (or hinder it). This often does away with many of the traditional company strengths normally brought forward by managers.

3. Many an internal analysis fails to evaluate of the internal situation, and thus is no more than a description of the organization. The main cause is internal company politics. Management should dare to be blunt while evaluating the company and its own performance for the sake of clarity and insight of the company's competencies.

5.4 THE SWOT(I) TOOL AND ITS APPLICATION

To remind us of the objective of the SWOT, which is to integrate the external and internal analyses and identify the company's strategic issues, we prefer to use the label SWOT(I) instead of SWOT. This will help us to remain focused. It also suggests that management should look beyond the obvious and identify salient 'issues'.

Although we ourselves prefer to identify 'strategic issues' based on a discussion and evaluation of the relationships between the list of external key developments/success factors and the main internal competencies rather than using a matrix, a full description of the steps involved in a sound SWOT(I) analysis is next. Also a brief example per phase is provided. We have found that keeping focused on generating salient strategic issues and allowing for iteration in the process to find them are key to a successful SWOT(I). Furthermore, the instrument benefits from learning by doing.

Figure 5.2: The five steps of the SWOT(I) analysis

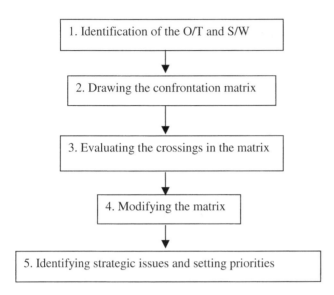

1. Identification of the O/T and S/W

2. Drawing the confrontation matrix

3. Evaluating the crossings in the matrix

4. Modifying the matrix

5. Identifying strategic issues and setting priorities

1. Identifying opportunities-threats and strengths-weaknesses:

The first step is identifying opportunities-threats (key success factors and developments) and strengths-weaknesses (competencies) based on the external and internal analyses respectively. For this step to be successful the external and internal analyses should have listed all significant key success factors and internal aspects.

Although initially considered to be separate, a certain level of iteration between external and internal analysis should be allowed for. Consider the following example. In the 1970s a well-known European audio manufacturer experienced a loss of market share. It identified a trend for new design in the marketplace. However, its management never decided to evaluate their company's design capabilities and kept focusing on technical quality and capabilities. Consequently, when the managers linked their set of significant trends to their company's strengths and weaknesses they never identified design as an important issue.

Some authors have suggested focusing on the main (say, 5) opportunities and threats. Others have suggested to factor analyze, i.e. condense them using a cross impact analyses (see Chapter 3). The latter approach may actually be the best as it is most focussed on identifying key success factors. The method consists of plotting trends on both axes of a matrix and figuring out how they affect each other. The objective is to identify the main forces in the environment. Another a good alternative is leaving the data reduction till later, when working the confrontation matrix. Data reduction at an early stage can be difficult.

2. Drawing the confrontation matrix:

Next, drawing a confrontation matrix putting the opportunities-threats on the horizontal axis and the strengths-weaknesses on the vertical axis. To make sure that the figure does not become meaningless or hard to read, choose your labels for both the trends and competencies carefully. They should be (a) indicative and (b) facilitate the linking with items from the opposite dimension. For example, a trend of decreasing market growth may be labeled as such but can also, in line with the concept of the product life cycle and shake out theory, be titled "increasing competition" or "increasing cost competition". The latter already points to the fact that companies with an unfavorable cost structure will find it more difficult to compete successfully for the future.

3. Evaluating the crossings:

After drawing the matrix one should evaluate the interactions between the internal and external dimensions. The objective of this step is to link the trends in the industry with the company. "Plusses" and "minuses" can be used. A double plus means "very positive", plus means "positive" zero is "neutral", minus "negative" and double minus is "very negative". In order not to blur the picture one should first focus on the most important relationships, i.e. identify the most important fits and mis-fits.

It is important to keep in mind that the most plusses should emerge in the strong-opportunity segment and the most minuses in the weak-threat segment. If this is not the case than generally one of the dimensions has been overrated (or the other one underrated). A horizontal or vertical pattern shows that no discriminating value has been assigned to the opposite dimension.

4. Modifying the matrix:

After identifying the most important interactions we can rearrange the items on the horizontal and vertical axes in an attempt to create clusters of plusses and minuses. What we in fact will be doing is placing related internal and external items together (compare factor analysis). The clusters of plusses and minuses that emerge represent the strategic issues. In addition we can sum up the scores of the columns and rows to get an overall impression of the balance between positive and negative influences in the matrix. We should also look at the overall distribution of plusses and minuses over the four quadrants. Heavy concentrations of minuses in the threat/weakness quadrant show severe problems and thus need for turnaround management type of actions. Heavy concentrations of plusses in the opportunity/strength quadrant show a more positive picture and opportunity for growth.

5. Identifying issues and setting priorities:

Generally 2 to 5 strategic issues will emerge. A quick check to test the quality of the issues is to link them to the initial problem definition, i.e. the starting point of the strategy process. Although it is possible that due to the analyses more detailed and better information has become available generally a relationship should be present. Any discrepancy between the initial and final problem should be analyzed carefully. Although the outcome of the SWOT(I) analysis is supposed to be superior, mistakes may have occurred. The gut feeling underlying the initial problem definition should always be taken seriously. Furthermore, we should anticipate that due to the more detailed analyses, more strategic issues will have been discovered. They should logically follow from and complement the strategic insight gained.

Next the strategic issues can and should be prioritized. This will prove useful when we later on in the process when we discuss strategy implementation.

Table 5.2 provides an example and illustrates each step of the process outlined above. Please note that the procedure is not or should not be seen as a mechanistic set of rules. Creativity, skill and iterations are necessary to make the tool work. Although many people associate the latter with subjective interpretation subjectivity should be minimized. Note that managers and students who apply the instrument to a case situation do tend to come up similar strategic issues. This supports the robustness of the tool.

5.5 PRACTICAL GUIDELINES

Identifying a company's strategic issues is the objective of each SWOT(I) analysis. As such the tool plays a pivotal role in the strategy process. When formulating a new marketing strategy, management needs to address these issues and design appropriate organizational actions. Different strategies can be used to address similar issues. Let us illustrate this using an example of a company facing a too high cost structure in a situation of severe and increasing competition. Its management can counter this problem directly via cost reduction or indirectly by redesigning its products in a modular way using, for instance, its strong Research and Development competencies. In other words, a defensive and/or offensive way can be used to increase efficiency and reduce cost. Strategic alternatives, and the choice between them, will be the subject of the next chapter.

What remains is to formulate some practical guidelines for undertaking a SWOT(I) analysis. These suggestions are presented in Table 5.3. Both the input of the analysis and the use of the tool itself are addressed.

Table 5.2: An example of a SWOT-matrix

Case:

A manufacturer operates in a market with decreasing growth rate. However, the market is still open to new, innovative products, i.e. with new attributes.

The company entered the market after a few large companies. Its Research & Development are excellent and the organization has proven skills as far as marketing is concerned. It has a good relationship with the local government and has a solid financial basis allowing for investment. Production is less well organized. Production efficiency is not a strong point. Logistics and purchasing are recognized to be weaknesses. Further there is quite a turn over in personnel, personnel management is –as indicated by top management-- fair and the organization's Management Information System is currently being developed and improved after remarks of an MBA trainee. Finally the product design of the company's product line is rated lower than that of the company's direct competitors. In a recent test between customers and non-customers a significant lower score was obtained.

---

issues

Matrix before modification

		OPPORT'Y	THREAT
		Customers open to innovative new products	Increasing competition, need for cost comps
STRENGTHS	Research & Development	++	
	Relationship local government		
	Financial situation	+	
	Marketing	++	
WEAK-NESSES	Efficiency		--
	Turnover in personnel		-/0
	Logistics		--
	Limited MIS		--
	Personnel management		0/-
	Purchasing		--
	Design	-	-

Matrix after modification

		OPPORT'Y	THREAT	Σ
		Customers open to innovative new products	Increasing competition, need for cost comps	
	Research & Development	++		2+
	Marketing	++		2+
	Financial situation	+		1+
	Relationship local government			
	Design	-		
	Efficiency		--	
	Logistics		--	
	Purchasing		--	
	Limited MIS		--	
	Personnel management		0/-	
	Turnover personnel		-/0	
Σ		5+/1-	10-	

90

Table 5.3: Suggestions for a successful execution of the SWOT(I) analysis

External analysis	Internal analysis
• Substantiate external trends with empirical data, i.e. facts • Do not only rely on past data but make a "weak signal" based forecast regarding the next couple of years • Evaluate each trend's <u>influence</u> on the industry or market and try to formulate each trend as a key success factor • Be selective and pay special attention to future key success factors in stead of current success factors	• Substantiate internal analyses with facts • Make sure the analysis is not just a description of current business. Dare to call weak "weak" and strong "strong". • Clarify the point of reference while identifying strong and weak points (e.g. 'compared to main competitor') • Be sure to focus on underlying competencies of value creation in stead of superficial company aspects.
SWOT(I) MATRIX	
• First plot the matrix and put <u>all</u> opportunities/threats and strengths/weaknesses on the axes • Check the levels of abstraction and do not confuse strengths with opportunities and weaknesses with threats • Use labels and pay careful attention to the names (preferably clear key success factors and competencies) used • Focus primarily on the most important 'links'	• <u>Keep in mind the objective</u>, i.e. identifying strategic issues (fits and mis-fits) • Work in an <u>iterative way</u>. Modify labels and add items when necessary based on new strategic insight that emerges • Always check the issues identified against the initial problem definition

5.6 NOTES

[1] Schnaars (1991), p. 32.

[2] Hill and Westbrook (1997).

[3] Day (1990).

[4] Based on Hill and Westbrook (1997).

[5] Grant (1991), p. 363-364.

[6] Day and Wensley (1988).

[7] Based on Day (1990)

CHAPTER 6

CHOOSING A VALUE POSITIONING: STRATEGIC OBJECTIVES, OPTIONS, AND CHOICE

Managers should be careful not to become too committed to a particular program too early in a process. In formulating a marketing strategy, the first step should almost always be to think widely about alternatives.

---Urban and Star
Advanced Marketing Strategy

6.1 INTRODUCTION

In the previous chapters we set the stage for strategy formulation. The outcome of the analyses has provided us with an understanding of the status quo of the company and the market's key success factors. Competitors and customers have been analyzed in general and in detail. This and other analyses of the external environment have helped us understand the market place and its trends define the requirements to compete successfully for the future. The company's situation has also been studied carefully and its strengths and weaknesses were defined using a core competence perspective. The analysis of the financial situation helped to determine our investment-slack.

The results from the external and internal analyses were joint together using the SWOT(I) analysis searching for matches and mismatches. In line with our definition of strategy and strategic problems we looked for those interactions between the company and its environment where the one "reinforces" the other. These interactions were identified as strategic issues and can have positive or negative consequences for the organization's future. These issues will be the backdrops against which the company's management should formulate its objectives and strategic options. The bottom line criterion for each option will be its ability to counter negative issues, i.e. the strategic problems, and make use of positive ones.

The opportunities for new value creation should be exploited to a maximum. This means challenging the rules of competition and thinking out of the box in an attempt to identify new roads to value creation based on trends in the environment and the company's unique competencies, i.e. strengths.

Before management can move toward thinking about strategic options it should first set the *company's objectives*. This should include an inventory of all the firm's stakeholders and their attitudes toward the company and its intentions. Some objectives and goals will be carried over from the past. Others may be substituted by new, more challenging ones better reflecting the company's ambition. Establishing the company's goals and objectives and accessing their acceptability for stakeholders is important. As Kotler (1998) puts it: "Goals tell where a business wants to go, strategy answers how it plans to get there". In other words, without a clear sense of direction it is hard to determine the "best route". After the company's objectives are clear strategic options can be generated and evaluated.

Note that middle (and lower) management will affect the setting of company objectives and search for strategic options. Strategy formulation is generally not a sequential and top down process but rather a complex of decisions in which strategic analyses and decisions mold together the formulation of objectives. Often strategy emerges in a combination of management sessions and day-to-day business.[1]

In this Chapter we will first address the formulation of a mission statement, followed by a discussion of how to set goals and objectives. Different levels of strategic options will be distinguished. Next we will provide an overview of strategic option and discuss the way to select and evaluate strategies. We end this Chapter, like every chapter, with practical guidelines for this phase of the strategy formulation process.

6.2 MISSION STATEMENT: GUIDING THE SEARCH FOR STRATEGIC OPTIONS

Mission statement is a popular concept in the management literature. It is generally associated with or placed at the beginning of the strategy formulation process. It concerns top management's ambitions and intentions for the company. Generally it is captured in a one or two lines that are communicated to employees and other stakeholders, such as shareholders and customers. A mission statement typically consists of four elements:[2]

1. it defines the company's domain or market,
2. it holds its business goals and objectives and thus its ambition
3. it states the company values as an employer and toward other stakeholders, and
4. sometimes it includes a basic strategic choice or hints concerning the choice of value positioning made.

Examples of mission statements are Hewlett Packard who mentions that it wants to be a frontrunner in printing/computer technology and innovation and MCI saying that it is *the* global Communications Company.

Why do some books put mission statement right up front and do we present it here? First, there is a lot of confusion regarding mission statements. It is a trendy concept with little empirical support for its importance. Second, there is no consensus regarding its role in strategy formulation. Although mission statement is related to the question 'What business are we in?' it really involves the question 'Where do we want to be?'.[3] It summarizes a company's ambition, domain and strategic course in a nutshell. The latter is important to help the implementation process and gain support. Note, however, that an up to date mission statement can only be formulated when management has a sound understanding of the company, its organization and its market. The current or a general mission statement thus may guide an initial external and internal analysis, but the final mission statement can only be formulated after they have been executed. Based on the results of these analyses a modification of mission statement may be called for. This is consistent with the different motivations for strategic analysis identified at the beginning of this book. In Chapter 2 we identified four reasons for strategic analysis or reorientation based on two dimensions. One dimension was the degree of the mismatch between the company and its environment. In the case of a serious mismatch a new (initial) mission should be formulated to guide the strategic analyses.

In summary, if the mission statement does not pass the test it should be reformulated or abolished all together. A new initial mission may direct the analysis. Only later in the strategy formation process a new mission statement can be formulated. When management decides on the mission statement for the future it can institutionalize its content in a formal statement, i.e. mission statement and communicated it to the rest of the organization and other stakeholders to facilitate strategy implementation.

6.3 GOALS AND OBJECTIVES

With the company's mission statement and the results from the SWOT(I) analysis in mind management should now set its goals and objectives for the company. Dependent on the level of strategic reorientation of the company the deviation from previous goals and objectives can be larger or smaller. Although they are related there is a difference between goals and objectives that is important to take into account:

An objective is an end that one aims for. It is qualitative in nature and has no date on it.

A goal is explicit, it is quantified and has a date on it. Goals are steps that lead to an objective.

Due to their broad and general nature objectives are thus more closely related to mission than goals. However, goals are the necessary tools for a company's management to plan and evaluate their efforts and plan the steps toward reaching the objectives. Goals are concrete and have a deadline. The use and usefulness of both goals and objectives in business can easily be demonstrated. A company may have as its objective to be market leader in market X. The goals that are formulated may be an increase of market share (volume) of 5% per year reaching a total market share of 45% in volume within 3 years from now.

Although many company objectives may be economic in nature (e.g. Return On Investment; Gross profits) a firm's amalgamation of stakeholders also causes an amalgamation in objectives. This explains why criteria like continuity, flexibility, being a quality employer, being a reliable trading partner, and good social citizenship are also popular primary or secondary objectives. Profits are rather *an* objective than *the* objective. Furthermore, the other objectives often help reach higher profits in the long run.

Objectives should not be set too high or too low; they should be challenging but reachable and not frustratingly high. The feasibility of the objectives should be evaluated in the context of the outcomes of the SWOT(I) analyses. When the objectives are not challenging management may fail to try and push beyond the obvious. As a result the company might loose ground to its more aggressive competitors. However, when the objectives are set too high they may be thought to be unobtainable and unrealistic. This will lead to frustration and may even cause alienation. Good objectives are clear, challenging and give direction to the company. Good goals are explicit and clarify the route toward the objectives set. An amalgamation of objectives should be present that calculates for the positive and negative powers from company shareholders. Making the shareholders and their impact explicit is an important top management task and often thought of too lightly.

Objectives and goals can be formulated at different levels in the company. Apart from the corporate level (compare mission), the business unit and operational levels are distinguished. At the corporate level general choices will be made regarding market and ambition. At the lower level these choices will be made explicit. The business level narrows down the objectives and plans while at the operational level they are developed and shaped into action plans. The latter should be so specific that sales, production and purchasing managers will know what to do but still experience enough flexibility, i.e. can make adjustments when necessary.

6.4 STRATEGIC OPTIONS

After setting the company's objectives in line with its ambition and domain definition management can start searching for strategic option. This should be done in the context of the outcomes of the SWOT(I) analysis. Viable options are characterized by helping accomplish the company's objectives and goals, but also taking into account its strategic issues. The latter can also be used as a check of consistency.

6.4.1 FRAMEWORK

Three levels of strategic options can be distinguished. In line with Johnson and Scholes[4] we will discuss the basis of a company's strategy, the direction of its strategic development, and the different routes to organize strategy execution (see Figure 6.1). Given our focus on strategic marketing issues we will use the business strategy level as the starting point of our discussion and work our way down. The corporate level is considered as *the context* in which strategic marketing formulation takes place.

6.4.2 BASIC CHOICE

At the top of the hierarchy of strategic choice is the choice of the basis of value creation and competition. Porter[5] has identified four strategic options, i.e. *cost-leadership, cost focus, differentiation, and differentiation focus* based on two dimensions, i.e. (1) cost leadership versus differentiation, and (2) focused versus unfocused. Porter argues that strategic management is all about making choices.

Figure 6.1: Framework of strategic options[6]

1. Strategic basis	high level of abstraction
• cost, differentiation, focus	
• operational excellence, product leadership, customer intimacy	
2. Direction of development	
• Growth strategies	
• Consolidation strategies	
• Turnaround strategies	
• Milking strategies/Retreat/Selling off strategies	
3. Way of execution	
• Autonomous development	
• Joint development/cooperation	low level of abstraction
• Acquisition	

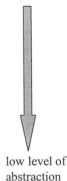

At the core is the decision to compete based on the lowest costs or the creation and delivering of unique products or services. The second dimension is whether the company tries to serve the market as a whole or just a particular segment. The latter option has a strong parallel with what others call a niche strategy.[7] Focusing or one or multiple niches only makes sense when there are barriers that make these segments a defendable part of the market. The company should aim to become a market leader (either cost or differentiation leader) in this segment.

Firms who do not choose one of the generic strategies face the danger of getting *stuck in the middle*. The logic is simple. When management chooses for a particular strategy it should stick to it and organize the total company, i.e. organization in accord with this strategy. Deviations or concessions will compromise the decision and create mediocrity in its customer value creation and thus market performance in the eyes of the consumer. By mixing options the company can easily be out performed by a "specialist" competitor that does not compromise its strategy.

In Porter's view barriers to entry and mobility barriers play an important role. Barriers often explain the roles that suppliers, buyers, substitute products and new entrants play in the market. They also help to explain an industry's overall profitability. Barriers of entry and mobility barriers thus are an important additional factor for understanding market dynamics. They explain why different *strategic groups,* i.e. groups of companies following different strategies, persist over time.

For a long period of time Porter's generic strategies have dominated strategic thinking. However, over the past decade the typology has become criticized. Although its generic strategies are still very useful for understanding many markets they are considered too simplistic. First, in many markets we find strategies that are hard to categorize as cost leader or differentiation; they seem to include elements of low cost and differentiation. Second, automation and computerization have increased the use of flexible manufacturing making the achievement of low cost while providing excellent service or customization just as possible. Third, companies that have adopted these new mix-strategies tend to belong to the most successful suppliers in their field (e.g. McDonalds, Levis, Toyota).

Whether it is wise to specialize on low cost or differentiation or to blend the two dependents on the question whether customer value is served or compromised by the decision. Porter's typology thus may still be a useful, but it may also be too limited for some markets. The core problem is that the typology is more supplier driven than customer driven, e.g. it focuses on low costs for the supplier rather than on low cost for the customer. It thus is limited as far as looking over the wall to the customer and analyzing product benefits is concerned. Consequently options such as hassle free delivery may be missed.

Still, although these comments a recent meta-analysis of studies about generic competitive strategy confirms that cost and differentiation are and remain the dominant strategic dimensions.[8] This is consistent with our perspective that the typology will be useful for many markets but not all markets.

Treacy and Wiersema[9] have set forward a strategy typology that is consistent with Porter's key dimensions of cost leadership and differentiation but that incorporates much better the value creation process toward the customer based on customer processes and seller-customer interactions (see Figure 6.2).[10] The authors see three alternatives for companies to compete in a marketplace: *operational excellence, product leadership, and customer intimacy.* Each strategy requires an organization that supports it, i.e. each strategy has its own organizational configuration. Although each strategy emphasizes a particular dimension of value creation for the customer each is characterized by at least scoring a minimal level of satisfaction on the other strategy dimensions. In other words, a product leader should have the best and most up to date products pushing the forefront of product technology, but it also needs to do this at a fair price (thus at acceptable production and handling cost). We will discuss the three strategies in detail next.

Figure 6.2: Basic strategies to compete for the future and their relationship

Porter (1980)	Treacy and Wiersema (1995)
• Cost leadership • low manufacturing cost, process R&D, efficiency	• Operational Excellence • low cost, more convenience for customer
	• Customer intimacy • close relationship with customer providing more customized solution
• Differentiation • unique products and services, top quality/technology, good marketing	• Product leadership • best, most innovative products at reasonable price
• Cost focus • Cost leader in particular market	
• Differentiation focus • Differentiation in particular market	
Assumption: make clear choice for cost or differentiation	*Assumption: focus on customer value and thus customer processes. Excel in one dimension but do not neglect the other dimensions*

Operational excellence

"Operational excellent companies deliver a combination of quality, price, and ease of purchase that no one else in their market can match. They are not product or service innovators, nor do they cultivate one-to-one relationships with their customers. They execute extraordinarily well, and their proposition to customers is guaranteed low price and/or hassle-free service.".[11] In other words, operational excellent companies are not simple cost leaders. Their focal point is not to lower their own production cost but rather to reduce their customers' overall cost levels. This requires a sound understanding of customer buying and production processes in order to be able to identify areas for further cost reduction at the customer. Lower overall customer cost may be reached through lower production cost and price, but may also benefit from adding services leading to hassle-free delivery at a slightly higher price.

Operational excellent companies have to manage their processes and organization for low cost and should keep track of overall customer costs/value. Four important organizational aspects are:

- A mechanism to ensure an end-to-end product and service supply that guarantees the lowest customer cost and is hassle free
- High standardization and simplification linked to tight control and a centralized type of planning
- Management systems that focus on integration and reliable, high-speed transactions complying with customer norms
- A low cost, low waste attitude and culture

An example of a company following this strategy is the United Chambers of Commerce in the Netherlands. The organization decided to become more cost efficient after the government privatized it. It saw that by making its unique company register and business information available on the Internet and using a single central telephone number rather than local numbers, it could lower its and its customers' costs considerably. The new set up provides customers with the latest information with 24-hour excess at an even lower rate than before. Use of the organization's database has rocketed and so have its revenues.

Product leadership

"A company pursuing product leadership continually pushes its products into the realm of the unknown, the untried. Its practitioners concentrate on offering customers products or services that expand existing performance boundaries. A product leader's proposition to customers is the best product, period".[12]   To accomplish this, a lot of creativity is required and willingness to cannibalize current products and processes. Entrepreneurship and intrapreneurship are important to be

100

able to identify and explore the "new". However, the company should also be able to commercialize its ideas quickly. This requires a good relationship between the technical and market side of new product development, and a good understanding of customers' openness to innovations, i.e. the innovators and early adopters in the market place.

Again four elements of the operational model of this strategic type are identified. Product leaders have:

- A focus on research and development, new product development and market exploitation.
- A rather organic organizational structure and processes allowing for entrepreneur and intrapreneur initiative.
- Management systems that are result and outcome driven. They stimulate experimentation and do not punish for it.
- A culture that encourages individual initiative and imagination and rewriting the market rules using innovation.

A company pursuing this strategy is Gillette. The company is continuously improving its shaving products. As such it sets the pace for competitors to react. However, it is also very strong in timing its new product introductions. Examples are the sequencing of double bladed shaving, adding a lubricated strip for more comfort, and introducing rubber ribs for improved beard-hair handling etceteras. 3M is another example of a firm with a product leadership strategy. In this company the reward systems are really promote intrapreneurship and the 'inventor' generally becomes the new product champion for further developing the idea and bringing it to market.

Customer intimacy

The third strategic option is customer intimacy. It concerns "[a] company that delivers value via customer intimacy builds bonds with customers like those between good neighbors. Customer-intimate companies don't deliver what the market wants, but what a specific customer wants. The customer-intimate company makes a business of knowing the people it sells to and the products and services they need."[13] These companies thus do not pursue transactions but cultivate relationships. A natural organizational structure for this type of company is to move more of the decision-making responsibility to the boundaries of the organization, close to the customer. Due to this customization approach customers become more loyal allowing for a higher margin for the supplier. Using trust the supplier persuades its customers to increase their investment in the relationship and become loyal. Features of the operational model of the intimate company are:

- A focus on solution development and relationship management
- A business structure and organization that delegates decision-making to employees close to the customer, e.g. account managers
- Management systems identifying and selecting high potential customers and researching ways to nurturing them
- A culture of customer specific rather than standard solutions, or making customers through relationship marketing feel special despite a standard or standard module-based solution

Take for example the value-added resellers SAP business software. They provide their customers with a complete business solution for managing their financial and other processes. The product is customized and tuned to their specific needs and requirements. This requires a sound understanding of the customers' processes and information needs. After installation it pays to nurture the relationship and stay close to the customer providing new additional solutions. This will prevent them from looking elsewhere.

6.4.3 DIRECTION OF BUSINESS DEVELOPMENT

After determining the basis for its strategy, and thus the focal point of the value to be created for the company's customers, management should determine where and how to build its position. Developing, holding, harvesting or engaging in turn around management may be needed. It thus concerns active portfolio management in the context of the generic strategy choices made.

Developing one's business requires a good understanding of the company's product-market portfolio. Because the company's resources will be limited choices will have to be made regarding where to invest and where to retreat. Again the objective is realizing the firm's overall objectives and goals.

Already in the 1960s Ansoff[14] identified four growth strategies looking at the interaction and potential interactions between a firm and its markets: the product-market matrix. He argued that company growth can come from penetrating the company's current market with improvement products, introducing new products for the company's current customers, finding new customers, i.e. new markets for its current products, and creating new products for new markets. He labeled these strategies *penetration* (line extensions and improvements of the company's current product line for the current market), *product development* (new products for the current market), *market development* (the company's existing products for new market segments and markets) and *diversification* (new to the company products for new market segments and markets), respectively.

Although the four paths identified are very useful they are limited in scope. They focus solely on growth. However, every manager knows that milking and deleting business activities or products are just as much part of the strategic decisions that have to be made. A more complete perspective on portfolio management also should include turnaround, holding and selling strategies.

Turnaround and retreat should not be seen as negative options per se. Cutting losses or freeing means and reallocating them are an important part of strategic reality and of many companies' life cycles. Much will depend of the total portfolio of the company and its stage of development.

Another modification of Ansoff's original typology is the broadening of the new product dimension. Based on the strategic arguments and strategic options formulated by Treacy and Wiersema product development should also comprise innovation of the customer's buying and internal processes. In fact, all innovation in products and services that can bring extra customer value should be considered. Figure 6.3 summarizes the paths of development discussed.

Figure 6.3: Directions for strategic growth[15]

Market Product	Current	New
Current	Penetration	Market development
New product/ augmented product	Product and service development*	Diversification

* from customer perspective including customer processes

It should be noted that the choices regarding the way of growth have a lower level of abstraction than the basic choice of strategy discussed earlier. Understanding the stage of development of the company and the strategies it has adopted for growth and development is important in order to understand the direction of development and potential ways still open to the company. The framework shows the total number of options open to management and the allocation problems it is facing.

6.4.4 DIFFERENT WAYS OF STRATEGY DEVELOPMENT

Finally, management should address the issue of how to realize the company's strategy. A company can try to realize its strategy autonomously, in cooperation with other organizations or via take over. Much will depend on the resources and time available.

Management and academic attention for this aspect of strategy formulation has increased significantly over the past decade. The notion that companies are part of a larger strategic network that determines to a large extend the firm's value has significantly changed the strategic landscape. Network thinking emerged after that many conglomerates, i.e. highly diversified firms, had lost touch with their markets and fell apart (e.g. AEG, Digital). In reaction to this many companies decided to focus again on their core competencies. They would stay in touch with developments in related and unrelated areas through strategic cooperation with other companies and organizations. This kind of partnering has several advantages, providing that the partners match each other well. It allows for flexibility and shared risk. Good examples are supplier-buyer strategic partnerships, exporting using agents, and Research & Development partnerships.

Together with the increased attention for partnering other strategic issues have also highlighted the question whether to use autonomous growth or joint development. First, the amount of money the development of new technologies requires has influenced make-or-buy decisions dramatically. Today attention is more focused on speed and flexibility than on solely owning a technology and protecting it. The protection often comes rather from keeping the pace of technological development high than from defending the turf, although much depends on the industry. Second, time and timing have become critical factors. It is reflected in the previous arguments regarding keeping up with technology but also plays a role in timing of market entry (e.g. foreign markets). Moving quickly has the advantage of more and better partners being available and distribution channels not yet being blocked by other international or global competitors.

The three strategic options of strategy-execution identified are thus part of a continuum with at the one end autonomous development or growth and at the other end acquisition. Cooperation with all its shades of gray is situated in the middle. The advantages and disadvantages of the three options will be discussed briefly.

Self-development is slow and rather expensive but has as an important advantage of management being in control. Sometimes the situation does not allow for autonomous development. The knowledge or means may be lacking or there may simply be not enough time for coming up with a new, competitive product oneself. An example is Kluwer Publishers whose stock lost 30% of its value when the company announced that it would invest some 100 million dollars in Internet activities to meet the challenge of e-business. Investors had no confidence in Kluwer's autonomous growth strategy based on lack of skills in the area. Further they probably thought the amount to little and that a lack of speed might hurt the company's competitive position with competitors' moving faster using acquisition strategies.

Cooperation and acquisition are more speedily strategies. Cooperation does not require a major investment or involved, although this is also considered its weakness. Cooperation is more flexible than acquisition although the revenues (and cost) also have to be shared. For both cooperation and acquisition a match in the partners' objectives and companies' culture is critical. Commitment of both parties is a key success factor for all 'joint' enterprises, as is good and clear leadership/management.

Although we can distinguish these three different options, the fact that they are located on a continuum does not mean that they all are readily available to a company. Much will depend on the situation and who is cooperating with who in the market already. The more cooperation is present the fewer candidates for cooperation may be left for our own company. Reputation is an important factor when trying to attract or find good partners.

6.5 GENERATING AND SELECTING STRATEGIC OPTIONS

6.5.1 GENERATING OPTIONS

After setting objectives and goals management should generate a number of strategic options that will help to accomplish them. This generating of options should be done with an *open mind*. In case of doubt it is better to include the option than to dismiss it too early.

The process of option generation requires creativity. Therefore, some form of brainstorming may be useful. The above framework can be used as a guideline. Thinking in accord with accepted rules and staying within boundaries is bound to be less rewarding than exploring new paths to create value. Good strategies challenge existing rules rather than that they accept them.[16] Often ideas come from copying approaches from other industries.

Options can be generated at all strategic levels identified. However, *the focus should be at the level at which the main strategic issues and problems are located.* This is critical in order to remain consistent and solve the problems at hand!

A strategic option can be seen as a road to a goal or objective. All plausible routes should be considered and evaluated. The degree of plausibility is determined by the nature of the problem or issue itself and the context of the SWOT(I) analysis. The danger of dismissing options too quickly is always present especially as managers think they know the problem, but are in fact biased because of narrow sightedness.

What is appropriate to include as plausible options can be illustrated by the following (static) example. Imagine your objective is to travel from London to Rome. Different options are available apart from the question, which route to take and when you need to arrive there. Options of traveling include going by car, train, plane, but also by foot, motorbike or bicycle or even by hot air balloon, space shuttle or rocket. In most scenarios the first alternatives will be evaluated and the latter will be dismissed up-front. The basic selection takes place based on basic criteria such as time available, effort, money and technical stance. These basic criteria and assumptions should be clarified to make clear why certain alternatives are left unspoken.

The option generation may focus on finding a solution to the company's main problem or issue but can and should also address the other issues identified. Consequently, a range of options will be generated. Again this has the advantage of looking beyond the direct strategic problems per se. Furthermore, it makes clear that there may be more problems that compete for management's attention. In the process of evaluating the strategic alternatives it will be possible to set priorities for the short term and long term and thus prioritize the strategic options available.

6.5.2 EVALUATING OPTIONS

To evaluate the options identified evaluation criteria need to be formulated. The idea is that an objective evaluation is better than a subjective and implicit one. The evaluation criteria and evaluation process should be transparent and based on sound arguments.

A good evaluation of strategic options uses a wide *range of criteria*, including the acceptability of the alternative for company stakeholders, use of the company's unique competencies, use of future opportunities for customer value creation etceteras on top of simple economic criteria as Return on Investment (ROI) and net profit.

In the literature three broad categories of clusters of evaluation criteria have been suggested: *suitability, feasibility and acceptability*. A good evaluation uses criteria from each *cluster*. The number and allocation of criteria over the clusters depend on the type of organization and the company's situation. For example, when it concerns a public organization or chemical company more items from the acceptability cluster should be drawn than for a small commercial food company. The social role or environmental issues make more attention for this category necessary. We discuss the clusters of criteria next.

Suitability

The cluster of suitability criteria includes two types of evaluation criteria. First, it includes the questions and thus items referring to the fit of the option with the outcomes of the SWOT(I) analysis. Examples are: Does the alternative solve the strategic problem? And, does it make use of opportunities in the market for creating new customer value? Second, it should help to evaluate the accomplishing of the company's objectives and goals. When no serious contribution is made, the option should be dismissed.

Please note that suitability is a very important cluster for the evaluation of potential strategies. Its criteria refer to the core quality of the alternatives. It ensures consistency along the line of future key success factors in the market, strategic issues, and value creation.

Feasibility

Except for checking the options' contribution in reaching our objective and making use of elements identified in our SWOT-analysis, we should check the alternative's feasibility. The latter has two dimensions. First, there is the option's internal feasibility. A company may lack the financial means, resources, skills or knowledge to execute it. This is the check from a core competence perspective. However, also external factors may be of influence. Finances and competencies should be evaluated with the company's main competitors and their strategic ambitions and reactions in mind. Furthermore, the element of time and timing should be included.

We may argue that the internal situation of the company determines whether the strategic option is feasible, whereas the external aspects determine of affect the degree of feasibility.

Acceptability

An organization is a cooperative of individuals with a set of joint objectives. This multitude of people acts in a network of stakeholders that consists of banks, the government etceteras. For these internal and external stakeholders options may be more and less acceptable. Accessing their attitudes toward a strategic option because they can help or hinder the option's implementation significantly. This cluster of evaluation criteria is thus of a political nature. Examples of items are, e.g. acceptability of an option for employees, acceptability for shareholders, and acceptability for environmental groups.

In the total evaluation process it is important to make sure to include items from each of these three clusters and to motivate carefully why the evaluation criteria selected have been chosen. When the criteria are selected the actual evaluation can take place. To ensure an objective evaluation it is useful to use a matrix that plots the options against the evaluation criteria and scores each option on each criterion. When desired different weights for each criterion can be used. Next per criterion a rating can be produced using plusses and minuses (--,-,0,+,++). To derive an overall judgement the scores can be summed up. The scoring should be accompanies by a careful motivation for each score and alternative in order to clarify the underlying assumptions and minimize subjectivity. Figure 6.4 shows an example.

| | OPTIONS | | |
CRITERIA	I. Market Development	II. Product development	III. Diversification
Suitability			
• solve marketing problem	+	+	++
• meet goals			
- 10% growth	+	+	+
- Customer retention	0	+	+
- Innovation	0	+	+
Feasibility			
• External feasibility			
- Competition	0	+	-
- Customer needs	+	++	+
• Internal feasibility	-	+	-
Acceptability			
• External stakeholders	+	+	0
• Own organization	+	+	-
Overall score	6+, 1-	10+, 0-	6+, 3-

When a single alternative is highly superior, one should question the evaluation's integrity. May be important options have been forgotten or the evaluation was manipulated in order to let a single alternative win. This sometimes happens consciously or unconsciously. Sometimes managers become committed early on in the strategy formulation process and then work toward this option. However, as the purpose of the planning process is to plan more objectively and to show the assumptions used, this needs to be recognized and challenged.

6.6 PRACTICAL GUIDELINES

Several suggestions can be made to help you with the SWOT(I) analysis.

1. Remain objective and take a stance. Do not put being diplomatic to your top management first.

2. Do not reach closure to soon when generating options. Think broadly and let yourself be inspired by the developments identified in the external analyses and particularly the vision on where the industry is going emerging from it. Keep in mind that when your options are too conservative the strategic value of your plan will be limited. Think out of the box and challenge strategic reality for the best results.

3. Try to sort or cluster the options identified using the three levels distinguished in this chapter. It will help you in two ways: (1) it will help to ensure consistency in

your plan, i.e. ensure that the options fit the strategic problems identified, (2) it will help to better understand the nature of your options and provide you with a check of completeness. When options of different strategic levels are included differentiate between these levels and make decisions for each level. Develop a perspective on differentiating between long and short-term solutions.

4. Do not only state the options but provide enough detail so that anyone can understand them. Furthermore the detailing will help to understand the nature and content of the option and not leave it hanging in the air.

5. Be sure to clarify the criteria for evaluating your alternative strategies. It should be clear why a certain option is chosen and others dismissed. Always check the level of fit between each option and the SWOT analysis. This will ensure making good use of your strategic analyses and its conclusions.

6. Although the method was described in a rather mechanistic style please bear in mind that only when used more organically, allowing for iterations, it will generate good results. Focussing on finding a match between the organization and its *future* environment rather than filling in checklists is a key success factor.

6.7 NOTES

---

[1] Mintzberg (1987).
[2] Sidu, Nijssen and Commandeur (2000); Bunt, Wijnia and Kloosterman (1994).
[3] Bunt, Wijnia and Kloosterman, (1994).
[4] Johnson and Scholes (1999).
[5] Porter (1980).
[6] Johnson and Scholes (1999).
[7] Kotler (1999).
[8] Campbell-Hunt (2000).
[9] Treacy and Wiersema (1995).
[10] Cambell-Hunt's study shows that archytypes such as marketing and operational leadership do exist and are related to cost economy types. However, excellence at the same time her results suggest -like we argue- that operational excellence types are more marketing, i.e. customer oriented. It is important to realize that cost leadership and operational excellence are related but somewhat different archytypes that may coexist in an industry.
[11] Treacy and Wiersema (1995) p.31.
[12] Treacy and Wiersema (1995) p. 35.
[13] Treacy and Wiersema (1995) p.38.
[14] Ansoff (1969).
[15] Source: Ansoff (1969).
[16] Hamel (2000).

CHAPTER 7

DELIVERING CUSTOMER VALUE:
EXECUTING MARKETING STRATEGY

'If we're not customer driven, our cars won't be either'
--- Statement by a Ford executive[1]

7.1 INTRODUCTION

Delivering customer value is as important as identifying value opportunities and choosing value positions. Activities related to actually enabling customers to obtain the value that is being offered by the firm, by means of their products and services, are moments of truth for any supplier firm. Thus, although the process of strategic analysis and strategic choice is crucial to identify value creation opportunities that may evolve into sustainable competitive advantage for the firm, the quality of executing marketing strategic choices, i.e., delivering the customer value is crucial for success in the marketplace.

Unfortunately, issues related to execution and implementation of marketing strategy often do not get the attention they deserve. In strategic marketing planning processes, often ample time is allocated to the analyses and SWOT, but marketing strategy execution is either completed in minimal time or receives no attention at all. Needless to say that this stimulates failure rather than success of the marketing strategy.

Making a strategy work consists of two main activities. First, identifying customer(s) (groups) to be served and determining how they will be targeted. The latter is accomplished by translating the decisions with respect to the firm's overall core positioning (i.e., the value definition) towards the specific customer group(s). The overall positioning for the organization has been chosen as part of the competitive strategy. Now, in the execution stage of the marketing planning process, this positioning has to be given meaning for each customer segment that will be chosen to be served. This means designing a marketing program with the use of instruments such as the marketing mix, that delivers the value that the organization chooses to offer in a way that is superior or unique compared to other suppliers and that satisfies the needs and benefits sought by its target customers. This process is also referred to as the tactical marketing process. Fortunately (and logically) market segmentation has already been performed as part of the external analysis. It will now be the starting point.

Second, the marketing program that is defined and the marketing tactics that have been chosen should lead to corresponding activities by members of the organization. Thus, the strategy that has been chosen and will be translated into a more detailed plan of marketing activities will have to be implemented within the organization in order to "get things done". This refers to the process of strategy implementation. It encompasses all organizational requirements to implement the strategic choices made by the organization. As such, it refers to issues such as allocation of tasks and budgets, implementing organizational changes, designing organizational structures, systems and processes in order to implement strategy, etceteras. The implementation process is discussed in Chapter 8. In the present chapter we will address the marketing program and the marketing plan that are aimed at executing marketing strategy and delivering the value to customers that the organization chooses to serve.

7.2 THEORETICAL BACKGROUND OF MARKETING EXECUTION

Traditionally, marketing has focused extensively on the execution of marketing activities aimed at serving customer needs. Much attention in the 1960's and 70's was devoted to identify the optimal mix of marketing tools or instruments that the marketer could use to target the customer market. The very well known "4 P's" introduced in the early 1960s by Jerome McCarthy based on earlier work by Neil Borden received substantial attention in the years thereafter, both among marketing practitioners and academics alike. So marketing has since long been paying significant attention to activities that relate to actually executing marketing decisions. This would make one think that marketing execution by means of formulating a marketing program based on a set of marketing instrumental activities as part of the overall strategic marketing planning process should be a piece of cake. Unfortunately, the contrary seems to be the case. As Nigel Piercy notes: "it is suggested that many of the problems faced in marketing implementation arise not simply from practical problems in management execution skills, but because conventional approaches to strategy development in marketing are based on the view that strategy development or formulation and marketing implementation are distinct and sequential activities".[2] Indeed, strategy formulation and marketing execution have suffered from a serious 'distance' between the two in the past.

As strategic planning became in vogue in the 1970s, strategy and marketing management evolved distinctively. Strategy was concerned with the formulation of long term strategic plans, whereas marketing dealt with formulating specific activities to target the customer market. The bridge between the two was essentially non-existent (see also chapter 1). This led two marketing academics, George Day and Robin Wensley, in 1983 to plea for a strategic approach to marketing.[3] In essence, they pointed out that marketing should be involved in strategy formulation too as it had to play an important role in two highly strategic issues: 'which markets should be served and what offer should be made to these customer markets?' (choice of business/market), and 'in what way are we distinctive from our competitors?' (distinctive advantage). These issues were not addressed by marketing management in a strategic way and were not translated into marketing activities by the strategists of the organization. At the same time these strategists became more and more aware of the importance to link strategic planning to management (leading to the emergence of strategic management). Consequently, the attention for bridging the gap between strategic choices and marketing management (execution of marketing activities) increased.

Marketers began to understand that an effective "translation" of strategic choices into specific marketing activities required that marketing instrumental choices were made interdependently and in concordance with the strategy formulated at the top of the organization. In order to accomplish such, awareness rose that market-related choices (such as which markets, or parts of markets to serve, and how) that directly follow from strategic choices at the corporate or business level should drive the marketing program (=the set of marketing instrumental activities to be deployed). Consequently, segmentation and market targeting became important tools. Segmentation helps to outline the specific customer needs the company intents to address and targeting serves to narrow down the market and particularly the business domain defined. Next, positioning serves to define and communicate the company's unique positioning vis-à-vis its competitors in the market. Segmentation, targeting, and positioning help to bridge strategy formulation on the one hand (the traditional 'strategic planning') and marketing execution (marketing program and plan; the traditional 'marketing management') on the other. In the next paragraph we will discuss how these concepts should be understood in the light of marketing strategy execution and we will discuss the content of the actual marketing execution process by means of the marketing program and the marketing plan.

7.3 CONTENT OF MARKETING EXECUTION

Marketing strategy refers to the way in which an organization chooses to compete on a specific market by means of a specific positioning. Thus, marketing strategic choices determine the value proposition that will be offered for the company's target customers. Execution of a marketing strategy then refers to the way that the value proposition will be delivered. If the organization chooses to target all customers in the market without differentiating between them and uses the same marketing program for everyone, it is using *undifferentiated marketing*. If, on the other hand, it designs and uses a separate marketing program for each market segment distinguished (or even sometimes for each customer) the organization uses a *differentiated marketing approach*. However, the company can also target only part of the market. It may for instance target a single, very specific segment. This is referred to as *focused marketing* or *concentrated marketing*. When special competencies are required to serve the segment we speak of a niche and thus a niche marketing strategy. Under these conditions the segment tends to have its own market leader and the type of competition is different from the market at large.

Factors such as segment size, segment growth, segment profitability (potential), current and potential competition, and the organization's own capabilities and resources will influence the company's decision regarding these alternative marketing strategies. [4] For example, small companies tend to specialize. Companies opting for a niche strategy often reduce risk by serving multiple niches. The portfolio analysis discussed in chapter 4 can help to identify interesting market segments.

Once market segments have been selected the organization should choose her positioning strategy. *Positioning* is the way in which an organization, brand, or product attempts to achieve a sustainable, financially attractive position vis-à-vis competitors that in the perception of the target customer is to be preferred over competing and alternative products, brands or organizations. A positioning has to be chosen for each target segment or customer that is to be served. In the event that the firm pursues an undifferentiated marketing strategy, this positioning will be identical for all segments/customers. The more the positioning is tailored to specific customer segments or even to individual customers the more differentiated the company's marketing effort and the more expensive its marketing program generally becomes. The choices made with respect to its positioning are generally described in detail in a *positioning* or *brand concept or statement*. It reflects the brand (or supplier's) *value proposition* ('why should I buy this brand/product?'). It forms the inspiration for programming the specific marketing strategies that are geared at delivering the customer value. The positioning statement serves as guideline for the marketing planning process at the tactical level. Therefore, in order for the positioning statement to be effective, it has to satisfy certain requirements. More specifically, a positioning should clearly:

- demonstrate the core value that the organization offers its customers
- demonstrate differences between the organization and its competitors
- be consistent, and
- be a meaningful starting point for executing the marketing program (this chapter) and implementing marketing activities (next chapter).

Based on the organization's chosen positioning, a marketing program is to be designed. For each segment or group of customers that the organization has chosen to differentiate its positioning for, such a marketing program will have to be developed. This includes formulating marketing objectives and goals and filling in the marketing mix consistent with the positioning. The *marketing mix* is a set of tactical marketing instruments that can be used to formulate a coherent set of marketing activities that enables the firm to deliver customer value that is consistent with its value proposition. Traditionally, the marketing mix has been described to consist of "4 P's", i.e. Product (the total product or service offer), Price (the monetary cost that the customer has to suffer to obtain the offer), Place (the means of distribution by which the offer is delivered to the customer and the process that enables this delivery), and Promotion (all communication and sales promotion activities with respect to the offer).[5] However, since its introduction, several additions to the marketing mix has been proposed. First and most importantly, the marketing mix has been extended to fit services, business-to-business, and retailing, and to make a clear distinction between structural aspects and promotional aspects with respect to each of the marketing instruments in the mix. In paragraph 7.4.1, we will discuss the marketing mix in more detail. Second, the marketing mix has been criticized for using a seller's rather than a buyer's perspective.[6] Alternatively, the four "C's" have been proposed that mirror the P's from a customer point of view:

Product	→ Customer value
Price	→ Cost for the customer
Place	→ Convenience
Promotion	→ Communication

This customer perspective stresses the customer value dimensions of the 4 P's. Customers are interested in the value offered to them rather than the product. Also, the costs that have to be incurred go beyond price as there are searching, acquisition, and usage costs. Furthermore, customers would like to obtain offerings in a way that is convenient and hassle free. In most cases, customers also prefer two-way communication rather than one-way promotional activities. Focusing on customer value rather than merely "selling products" is the view any marketer should take. One should realize that product attributes are only the means to satisfy the benefits sought by the customer, not the end.

In sum, executing marketing strategy involves *decisions with respect to market positioning, marketing programming and marketing planning,* based on market segmentation research and target marketing decisions. The last two activities are part of the strategic marketing planning process and relate to the stages of strategic analysis and strategic choice, respectively. In Figure 7.1 the process is visualized.

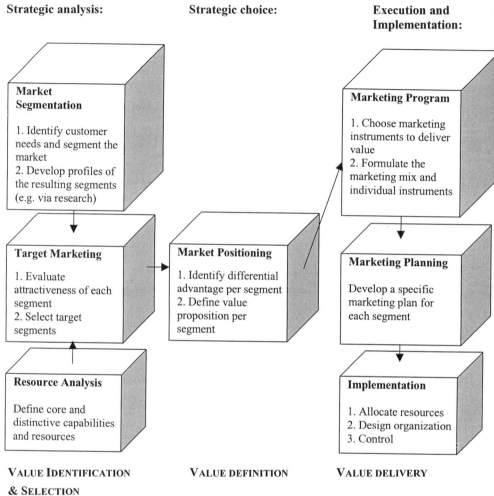

Strategic analysis: Strategic choice: Execution and Implementation:

Market Segmentation

1. Identify customer needs and segment the market
2. Develop profiles of the resulting segments (e.g. via research)

Marketing Program

1. Choose marketing instruments to deliver value
2. Formulate the marketing mix and individual instruments

Target Marketing

1. Evaluate attractiveness of each segment
2. Select target segments

Market Positioning

1. Identify differential advantage per segment
2. Define value proposition per segment

Marketing Planning

Develop a specific marketing plan for each segment

Resource Analysis

Define core and distinctive capabilities and resources

Implementation

1. Allocate resources
2. Design organization
3. Control

VALUE IDENTIFICATION & SELECTION   VALUE DEFINITION   VALUE DELIVERY

(SEGMENTATION → TARGETING → POSITIONING → PROGRAMMING → PLANNING → IMPLEMENTING)

In the Chapters 3 through 6 we discussed the process by means of which an organization can identify value opportunities by carefully segmenting and analyzing the market (Chapter 3), relating this to the organization's resources and capabilities (Chapter 4), thus enabling the firm to make adequate strategic choices in the light of their objectives (Chapters 5 and 6). In the following paragraphs of this chapter we will further address the process of value delivery (*marketing programming and planning*) based on value definition choices. Chapter 8 will addresses the *implementation* of the marketing plan and organizational and financial implications of the choices made.

7.4 INSTRUMENT TO USE: THE MARKETING (EXECUTION) PLAN

Next, we will discuss the marketing plan as an instrument to execute the marketing program. Although the marketing plan is not an instrument similar to the tools we discussed elsewhere in this book, it is a useful format to help formulate systematically a marketing program and drawing up a marketing execution and implementation plan. First, we will address the marketing program that should be formulated based on the positioning strategy/statement (7.4.1). Second, we will review the contents of the marketing plan. We will introduce a guideline for detailing and executing value delivering marketing activities (7.4.2).

7.4.1 THE MARKETING PROGRAM

The objective of marketing programming is to design a set of marketing activities that delivers customer value in a way that it is consistent with the organization's positioning strategy (value definition) for the customers they serve. Therefore, the first issue an organization has to address is to what extent marketing programming should differentiate between customer segments, depending on the heterogeneity of customer groups served and value propositions defined. Next, the organization has to decide on the specific types of marketing activities to use in communicating and delivering their offerings. This first requires choosing the marketing mix to be used. As we defined in the previous paragraph, the marketing mix refers to a <u>coherent set of marketing activities</u>. It includes identifying the different instruments that are available to the firm. Generally, the company will try to find the most effective instruments and select them for its 'tool kit'. Second, the instruments should be aimed and attuned to one another in order to create a consistent set of activities with a mutually strengthening (and synergistic) effect. Thus, a consistent and integrated marketing program is designed. It should effectively deliver and communicate the company's value proposition to its target customers. Let us illustrate this idea with an example.

In the late nineteen eighties, the *Toyota* company decided to manufacture and market a car in the luxury car segment: the *Lexus*.[8] This was a market segment that Toyota traditionally did not serve. As Toyota realized that their brand image at that point in time was formed by the cars they had previously marketed, the company decided to market their luxury cars with a new brand name. However, Toyota probably would not have been as successful with their new brand as they were in case they had not also changed the marketing activities for the new brand dramatically. Toyota's traditional success was based on marketing reliable quality cars at very competing prices in the mass-market car segment (especially compact cars). Although they held on to this core positioning (reliable quality cars at competing prices), the marketing mix for the Lexus was a totally different one from the marketing mix of Toyota's other cars. Realizing that Lexus had to succeed in the luxury car market, Toyota attracted new car dealerships that were characterized by high levels of personal attention and service towards the customer. Also extensive guarantee was offered on the product in order to stress

117

the high quality and reliability aspect. The price was also set highly, but at a competing level against competitors such as Mercedes and BMW. The essence of Toyota's success with respect to Lexus can largely be attributed to the choice and the degree of consistency between the instruments of the marketing mix that are deployed. First, Toyota carefully selected the marketing instruments to be used; personalized customer relationship management was one of the key instruments in their marketing program. Also their product offered significantly more value for money than other competing offers. Technically, the product was among the most advanced. Second, the marketing mix instruments were carefully attuned to one another. For example, new distribution outlets that matched the new brand's positioning were developed to market the product. Communication activities and media were designed to match the positioning. In sum, based on their core positioning of reliability and quality at competing price, Toyota successfully developed a new brand for a new customer segment and used its positioning as both starting point and binding factor for a new mix of marketing instruments. Such a mutually consistent set of marketing instruments is representative of a true marketing "mix" rather than a bundle of decisions on separate marketing instruments. This illustrates the pivotal role of positioning in formulating any marketing program.

In formulating a marketing program a firm has to address two different decisions. First, the organization has to decide on the marketing instruments to be deployed in the marketing program. Toyota, for example, included personal relationship management in its marketing mix for Lexus, whereas this instrument played a lesser role in its mix for Toyota cars. Second, the organization has to carefully attune the marketing instruments. The example shows how Toyota developed two different brand images creating synergy between its brands, products and organization meeting the increasingly important need for a coherent marketing mix.

An organization should be aware of potentially relevant sets of marketing instruments that can be deployed. Below, we will discuss the most popular sets that have been proposed in the literature.

7.4.1.1 THE 4-P FRAMEWORK

The traditional set of marketing instruments, introduced in the early nineteen sixties (by Jerome McCarthy based on earlier work of Neil Borden), refers to a framework of four "P's": Product, Price, Promotion, and Place (Distribution).

The *'Product'* refers to the organization's most important marketing instrument, i.e. its *offering* to customers aimed at satisfying their needs. As such, it is the representation of the core proposition that the firm offers to the market. Therefore, it also is an important means for the organization to differentiate itself from the competition. It should be understood that the 'Product' is more than a physical product. It also refers to services ('service products'), but also captures the different levels of the offering. Following Theodore Levitt's well-known classification of products, it includes the *core product* (the core benefit offered by the product that relates to the core need that the product satisfies), the *tangible product* (the physical product that is being offered or the tangibles in the case of services), and the *augmented product* (that refers to the tangible product supplemented with all additional services—'product services'—such as product guarantee, financing and so forth).

When formulating the marketing instrument of 'product', firms should consider the decisions regarding all three levels. Decisions related to product innovation, elimination, and modification are part of the marketing instrument also.

Just like all marketing instruments 'Product' consists of a sub-set of instruments. With respect to 'product' decisions the following aspects can be distinguished:

- product variety   - packaging
- quality   - design
- features   - brand name
- sizes   - services
- warranties   - returns

'Price' refers to the costs that customers have to bear to acquire the organization's offering. It generally refers to the list price of the product, but may include additional pricing schemes such as bundled pricing (the –often discounted—price of products when obtained in a bundle rather than separately), add-on pricing (prices of additional, supplementary products), promotional pricing (special offers, discounts, allowances), differentiation pricing (different prices for different market segments, time instances etceteras), and psychological pricing (appealing prices –such as EUR 5.99 instead of EUR 6.01—or prices to reflect the image—such as rounded prices, e.g. EUR 75.000 for a luxury car rather than EUR 74.999). Also decisions with respect to payment periods and credit terms are part of this marketing instrument. Three basic pricing strategies are distinguished. Firms may follow one or any combination. First, many organizations choose to set their prices (largely) based on the costs they incur. In case of these *cost based pricing* methods mark-up percentages are added to include the desired profit (or return on investment) in the list price. It goes without saying that such a pricing method does not take into account any market conditions. High cost levels are reflected in high list prices. Although it may seem strange from a marketer's point of view, cost based pricing is still very popular among firms. It is probably its objectivity and simplicity that contributes to this high level of penetration.[9] Other pricing methods that do take market conditions into account include *competitor based pricing* and customer based pricing. In case of the former, competitors' prices are the point of reference for the organization's price setting. With *customer oriented pricing*, customer price perception and customer demand are taken as the starting point for the company's price setting. More recently, attention for *value based pricing* has increased. Here the prices are set based on customers' perception of the value of the offerings in the market.

The decisions with respect to *'Promotion'* cover a broad spectrum of communication activities and instruments. This marketing instrument includes five broad classes of marketing instruments, i.e., *Advertising, Sales promotion, Public Relations (PR), Sales force,* and *Direct*

Marketing (DM). Table 7.1 shows examples of different promotion tools that relate to each of these five promotion instruments.

Table 7.1: Promotion instruments and their tools[10]

Advertising	Sales Promotion	Public Relations
Print and broadcast ads	Contests, games, lotteries	Press kits
Packaging	Premiums and gifts	Speeches
Motion pictures	Sampling	Seminars
Brochures/booklets	Fairs; trade shows	Annual reports
Posters/leaflets	Demonstration	Sponsoring
Directories	Coupons	Publications
Billboards	Rebates	Community relations
Displays	Low-interest financing	Lobbying
	Trade-in allowances	Company magazine
		Events
Sales Force	**Direct Marketing**	
Sales presentations	Catalogs	
Sales meetings	Mailings	
Incentive programs	Telemarketing	
Samples	Electronic shopping	
Fairs and trade shows	TV shopping	
	Fax mail	
	E-mail	
	Voice mail	

In essence, promotion instruments are communication activities that are aimed at affecting any (combination) of the stages in the customer's decision making process. In general, three stages are distinguished that may be subject to targeting by communication activities. These include the stages of knowledge (cognition), feelings (affection, emotion), and action (behavior). Of course, each stage can be subdivided in sub-stages in order to reflect the buying or decision making process more realistically. The communication instruments available to the organization differ in their effectiveness per (sub-) stage. Therefore, dependent on the communication objectives, the firm should carefully select and use these instruments.

Finally, *'Place'*—or better: distribution—refers to all instruments that are available to an organization in order to deliver the offering to the customer. This market instrument relates to two kinds of decisions. First, the organization needs to consider how products and services are physically distributed to customers; this relates to the *supply chain*. Second, the supplier needs to decide what marketing activities which parties in the marketing channel will cover. Note that physical distribution activities need not coincide with marketing activities. Wholesalers, for example, often primarily have a distribution function, whereas some Internet retailers may predominantly have a marketing function. A basic decision that needs to be addressed is whether the organization will choose to serve customers in a direct or indirect way (using middlemen). Place decisions include issues such as: channels to be used, market coverage, assortments, locations, inventory, and transport.[11]

7.4.1.2 ADDITIONAL P'S: POLITICS AND PUBLIC OPINION

Philip Kotler proposed to add two P's to the traditional framework, especially to reflect the increasing importance of global marketing. These include *'Politics'* and *'Public opinion'*. The former refers to political activities, such as lobbying, that can have an important effect on the organization's marketing effectiveness (e.g., in the case of tobacco companies). The latter P relates to the influencing of moods and attitudes of the general public that severely can affect consumption (e.g., public opinion on alcohol consumption).

7.4.1.3 THE 7-P FRAMEWORK OF SERVICE COMPANIES

Especially for organizations selling services, i.e. delivering customer value through service provision, three additional marketing instruments have been proposed to play a vital role. These include Processes, Physical evidence, and Personnel. *'Processes'* refer to the service provision process, including the procedures used to deliver the company's services to its customers and the interaction process between supplier and customer. As the customers participate in the service delivery process they have a large influence on its (perceived) level of quality. Understanding and optimizing the service delivery processes is important to achieve customer satisfaction. *'Physical evidence'* relates to the tangibles that are part of the value delivery process. Although a service is (largely) intangible tangibles can often be used to physically support the service and/or signal certain service quality levels (e.g. waiting room). *'Personnel'*, finally, refers to the actual providers of the service. Since they determine the customer's service experience to a large extent, personnel is a key marketing instrument in customer value delivery. Generally a distinction is made between front and back office.

Increasingly all organizations are considered some sort of service company. In order to deliver customer value that is differentiated from and superior firms need to be highly customer oriented. In order to implement such a customer orientation effectively, the marketing instruments that have been used in the context of services marketing have proven to be most effective. They play an important role when the goal is not only to satisfy the customer, but to delight the customer.[12] The reason is that the 7-P framework involves the company as a whole, and via the variable 'personnel', includes internal marketing.

7.4.1.4 From marketing program to marketing plan

Once the organization has decided on both the general and specific set of marketing instruments to be used in executing the marketing program and in what ways these instruments should be interdependent, a more concrete plan of executing the proposed marketing activities can be developed. Such a plan should be developed for every market segment that will be targeted in a differential way. The marketing plan is the subject of the next paragraph.

7.4.2 The Marketing plan

A good tool to ensure adequate attention for marketing strategy execution and implementation is the marketing plan. The marketing plan concerns a detailed planning of the activities that are part of the marketing program, which results from the marketing strategic choices made earlier in the marketing planning process, particularly the targeting and positioning. The plan should start by summarizing the strategic choices made and stating the overall marketing objectives and goals the company will pursue (e.g. 40 percent market share in 2 years). Next the marketing tactics and operational activities need to be developed for the planning period. It should be accompanied by an implementation plan in order to facilitate its execution. Here we will focus on the content whereas the implementation will be discussed in Chapter 8.

Using the strategic summary as an inspiration and guideline the marketing instruments need to be filled in aiming for a coherent mix. Using a similar structure per instrument is useful. It will keep the plan transparent and make it easy to check for completeness. Also each instrument's contribution to the overall marketing goals and objectives will be helped as they are individually specified.[13] To further each instrument's role the following aspects should be addressed for each instrument:

- *Objective:* what is the objective that this particular marketing instrument should satisfy (also in relation to the more general marketing objectives and the objectives of other marketing instruments in the mix that is chosen)?
- *Strategy:* in what way should this instrument achieve its objective and how does this co-align with the overall strategic choices (especially the value definition and market positioning)?
- *Execution:* what specific (tactical and operational) activities need to be undertaken in order to execute the strategy for this particular marketing instrument?
- *Control:* how is the effectiveness of this particular marketing instrument in achieving its objectives measured?

This will result in the formulation of different plans for the specific marketing instruments that will be deployed. Thus, a product plan, communication plan, and distribution plan are developed.

In addition to the detailed formulation of the individual marketing instrument plans, a detailed comment should be made with respect to how the instruments complement each other in general and over time in particular, allowing for synergy. This will help the marketing instruments to form a coherent mix of marketing activities that can be orchestrated in such a way as to effectively deliver the customer value as defined in the firm's corporate or business strategy and positioning statement. Table 7.2 summarizes the key elements in the (annual) marketing plan as discussed. The latter part relates to the implementation plan of the marketing strategy, its financial implications and control, will be discussed in the next chapter.

Table 7.2: The key elements of the (annual) marketing plan

MARKETING PLAN
I   **Strategic Summary** *Strategic audit: opportunities for value delivery* → most significant opportunities and threats → most significant resources and capabilities (strengths and weaknesses) → strategic issues *Strategic choices: value definition, market targeting and positioning* → competitive strategic choices → growth strategy → target segments → positioning (overall and per segment in case of differentiated marketing strategy)
II   **Marketing Mix** *Choice of marketing instruments to be deployed* *Interdependency of marketing instruments and their relation to the overall value definition and core proposition*
III   **Marketing Instruments** *Explicit formulation per marketing instrument for each separate target market:* - Instrument's objective - Instrument's strategy - Instrument's execution plan - Instrument control
IV   **Marketing Strategy Implementation** *Organizational changes* *Organization structure* *Resource allocation*
V   **Finance**
VI   **Control**

The strategic summary is a representation of the outcomes of the strategic (external and internal) and SWOT-analyses and the choices made in the strategy formulation stage. They are covered in detail in the comprehensive overall *strategic marketing plan*. Here, in the annual *marketing plan*—as the major plan of the execution and implementation stage—a summary of the strategic fundamentals suffices.

Planning of the marketing mix and the marketing program are at the core of the annual marketing plan. Although strategic fundamentals may not change yearly, marketing programs are more open to change—depending, of course, on the rate of change within the organization and its environment such as competitive actions and reactions. As the marketing program is the actual execution of the marketing strategy, it is of primordial importance that the marketing plan provides a detailed outline of the marketing activities that will have to be executed. They need to be updated regularly. Experience has shown that many organizations pay ample attention to the strategic analysis and choice phases, but hardly care to translate marketing strategic choices into actionable strategic marketing programs and plans. Too often the execution is inconsistent with the analyses and choices. Consistency and the formulation of a coherent program should be the focal point. In case the organization pursues a differentiated marketing strategy, each segment should be targeted separately. We will illustrate this process below for the traditional marketing instruments (the "4 Ps").

Consider an organization that has chosen to target two main customer segments. The benefits sought by consumers in both segments vary and so does their buying behavior. Therefore, a differentiated marketing approach seems called for. In the strategic marketing planning process, strategic choices regarding the value that the organization will offer to its customers will have to be defined as well as competitive, growth, and development strategies. Also marketing goals need to be specified. Now, these strategic choices are to be specified into actionable marketing programs. That requires that, given the positioning statement of the firm, plans for the organization's offering, pricing, promotion, and distribution should be developed. We will illustrate this by means of a fictive example. Consider a hotel that wishes to grow by offering hotel facilities to business and holiday customers in Europe.

Key starting points are: (a) the marketing strategic choices made and the specified level of growth as this will determine what the organization will and will not do, and (b) information on customers and competitors that is obtained in the external analysis as this will provide necessary input for formulating the marketing instruments.

(a) Strategic summary (choices):

- *Target market*: the hotel chain wishes to target both holiday makers and business customers in Europe.

- *Positioning*: the hotel chain offers superior customer value by providing high quality service at competitive prices, personalized attention to customers, high quality locations—but not in the most busy areas.

- *Marketing goals*: 15 and 22 percent market share in two years time for the two segments, respectively.

- *Competitive strategy*: the organization pursues a differentiation strategy (key differentiators: product offering, customization, location).

- *Growth strategy*: market development and penetration.

- *Development strategy*: internal (own funding) and by means of acquisition.

(b) Key customer & competitor information*)

Segment :	'holiday makers'	'business people'
Customer profile	-Young singles & couples -Families**)	Managers 35-55 yrs. old
Key benefits sought	Relatively low cost, fun, entertainment	Efficiency, convenience, privacy, comfort, support, empathy
Buying behavior	Makes own reservation Sometimes no reservation May consider range of alternatives ….	Reservations made by secretary Always make reservation Is likely to have short list ….
Competing offerings	Many differentiated alternatives	Well known, comparable, chains (e.g., Hilton, Sheraton)

*) For the sake of the example only minimal exemplary information is provided here; normally, the customer and competitor information –although briefly summarized here—will be more comprehensive.

**) These groups could be considered as separate segments in the marketing program as their needs and benefits sought probably differ significantly.

The strategic summary indicates that the marketing instruments of product, price, personal relationships, and distribution (=location in this example) play an important role. This choice of instruments and their interdependency together form the relevant marketing mix for the organization. This can be depicted as in Figure 7.2.

Note that this marketing mix refers to the marketing instrumental choices for the overall market to be served. Specific formulation of the contents of each instrument will require adjustment to the specific requirements and characteristics of each market segment that is targeted.

Figure 7.2: The Marketing *Mix*—Example

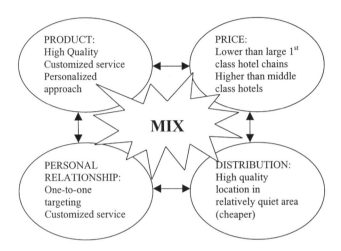

The choice of marketing instruments and the way in which they relate to each other constitutes the marketing mix. Although a plan will be formulated for each marketing instrument the plans are and should be interrelated and thus should refer to one another. As we indicated in this chapter, four basic items need to be addressed when formulating an execution plan for marketing instruments. First, the objective of the marketing instrument needs to be specified. This means that it should be clear what purpose the marketing instrument will serve in the light of the overall marketing objectives and marketing strategy. Second, the instrument strategy needs to be outlined. This refers to the way in which the instrument will achieve its objective. For example, the objective of price may be 'maximizing revenue'; this may be achieved by a pricing strategy of premium price levels. Third, an execution plan for the instrument needs to be drawn up. What exact price levels are going to be set; when will prices be lowered or raised; what discount policy—if any—will be followed, and so forth. Fourth, the parameters to measure the effectiveness of the instrument in achieving its objectives need to be outlined.

We will continue with a plan for a single marketing instrument in order to illustrate the above mentioned steps. As product is at the core of the value adding process we will focus on the product plan.

Product Plan

A product plan consists of the following elements:

- Product objective
- Product strategy
- Content of the offering
- Control measures (measurement of effectiveness)

Product objective

The objective of a marketing instrument should drive the decisions that are taken with respect to it. With respect to the objectives, one should think of the primary goals that are to be achieved by the instrument 'Product'. First of all this refers to the core benefits of the product for its target customers. In detailing the product objective, these benefits need to be explicitly formulated in order to prevent marketing myopia.

For the example of the European hotel chain the following **product objectives** might be:

Segment 'holiday makers': The product objective is to provide high quality accommodation services that are perceived to be customized to the individual guest and that trigger a sense of fun.

Segment 'business people': The product objective is to provide high quality—no nonsense accommodation to the experienced and demanding business traveler that is perceived to be customized and is generally located in other areas than the major business hotels.

Product strategy

In essence, the product offered by the firm represents the value that the organization aims to provide its customers. Thus, in the event that the organization has the objective to provide products that are to be perceived of high quality, the product strategy should reflect this. The product strategy provides the supplier's response to benefits sought by customers by means of specific choices with respect to the value offered. As customers evaluate a product based on salient attributes and their related benefits a characterization at the attribute level would be appropriate. This will also facilitate controlling for different segments served by different value offerings. It will be easy to indicate the attributes that have particular appeal for certain segments. Product strategies for the segments that are to be served by the hotel chain in our example might look as follows:

Product execution

The product strategy is given concrete meaning by detailing the offering in a product execution plan. It relates to the specification of the core, tangible and augmented product. All aspects of the product, including packaging, brand name, service augmentations, and so forth should thus be included in the product execution plan. Service products should be described in detail including both tangibles and intangibles.

Product control

The final element of the product execution plan as part of the marketing (execution) plan concerns the formulation of control measures in order to test the effectiveness of the product plan used. These control measures should therefore be directly reflective of the objectives with respect to the particular instrument—here, the product. For example, if the organization chooses to formulate product objectives in terms of product quality, evaluation measures with respect to perceived or realized (technical) quality need to be developed and used. Customers can be asked to rate the quality of the value offered; the amount of complaints can be registered; quality measures can be used to evaluate technical quality (such as percentage of come-backs etc.) and so forth. Some examples for product control measures for the example of the European hotel chain are given below.

Product control—example

The effectiveness of the product strategy in achieving the product objectives by the hotel in our example can be evaluated by measures such as:

- Customer satisfaction
- Customer's perceived degree of product (service offering) customization
- Frequency and nature of customer complaints
- Customer loyalty (repeat purchase rate)
- Customer evaluation of specific items such as hotel location, specific services
- Degree of customers that visit based on word-of-mouth information
- Etc.

Obviously, it would be insightful to differentiate these measures for the different segments served.

With the completion of all instrumental plans, the marketing program has been specified and is ready for implementation. The issues involved in the implementation process will be discussed in the next chapter.

7.5 PRACTICAL GUIDELINES

We conclude this Chapter with some practical guidelines to successfully formulate a marketing execution plan.

1. Remember that the marketing strategic plan is as strong as its weakest link. In practice the weakest link generally concerns the way the strategic choices are "translated" into a marketing program and marketing plan. Make sure that the execution gets enough attention and is consistent with the analysis and choices made. A good strategy is great,

making it work even greater! Check repeatedly whether the marketing program and the marketing plan are still formulated and executed in such a way that they are optimally geared to make the marketing strategy work.

2. Always use a systematic approach to marketing programming and planning. This will prevent you from forgetting important decisions within and aspects of the marketing execution.

3. Be creative! This means that one should not fall back on the traditional, well-known marketing instruments too much, too soon. Marketing has more to offer than the 4 P's. Furthermore, the most successful companies have in common that they are characterized by the adoption of new ways of distribution, new ways of presenting their products and so forth.

4. Be sure to address the interdependency between the marketing instruments and activities in the marketing (program) execution plan. Without it it is unlikely that your program will be consistent and will achieve synergies.

5. Make use of the results of the external analysis when formulating your marketing plan. In the external analysis you will find the answers as to who is buying, which products, why, and when. Using this information is not only helpful when aiming your marketing instruments, it will also help the consistency of your planning effort.

7.6 Notes

[1] In: Kotler (1999).

[2] Piercy (1998), p. 225.

[3] Day and Wensley (1983).

[4] See e.g., Doyle (1998).

[5] See e.g., Van Waterschoot and VandenBulte (1992).

[6] See Kotler (1999).

[7] Partially adapted from Doyle (1998).

[8] Production of Lexus cars for the domestic market began in May 1989 (www.global.toyota.com).

[9] Frambach, Nijssen and Van Heddegem (1997).

[10] Adapted from Kotler (1999), p. 107.

[11] Kotler (1999).

[12] See Rust, Zahorik and Keiningham (1996).

[13] Leeflang (1994).

CHAPTER 8

ORGANIZING FOR DELIVERING CUSTOMER VALUE

'It is no trick to formulate a strategy, the problem is to make it work'.

Igor Ansoff, Corporate Strategy

8.1 INTRODUCTION

Although the organization has now chosen its marketing strategy and detailed it in its marketing program and plan, several things still can go wrong. No strategic marketing plan has much influence when never executed. A sound implementation is thus required in order to prevent "the all too frequent failure to create change after seemingly viable plans have been developed".[1] Therefore, we will address the question *of how to implement the marketing effort.* Another reason is that despite ample attention for strategic marketing management in the literature, we observe relatively little attention for execution and implementation issues of marketing strategy.[2] We will point out and discuss the decisions to make and hurdles to take when implementing the marketing plan.

We will focus on two aspects. First and most importantly the implementation of the marketing plan itself. How does management organize the company and its people to realize the plan made, and when and how should the results be evaluated and controlled? Such an implementation requires making things happen. Apart from allocating means it requires motivating and mobilizing people. People and their communications *are* the organization. Second, there is the more general issue of the marketing function and the marketing department's position in the organization. Understanding this position and its evolution is important. The degree to which the organization is market oriented affects the ease or difficulty encountered in implementing the new strategic marketing ideas. It is the backdrop against which the marketing planning process takes place.

8.2 THEORETICAL BACKGROUND OF MARKETING IMPLEMENTATION

8.2.1 HISTORICAL GAPS

There are three causes for many of the problems experienced when implementing a marketing program.

First, it can be argued that traditionally the focus of strategic thinking has been on content rather than process and thus implementation. With strategic management it became clear that strategic fit could only be ensured when the strategic function is well integrated in the organization with also middle and lower management involved. The organization and its members needed to be motivated and well equipped to develop the added value identified and thus create the company's strategic position its top management desires. Strategic management evolved and the importance of internal communication and implementation issues were stressed. Although traditionally seeing implementation as an activity following strategy formulation and emphasizing organization design and the manipulation of systems and structures, it has now adopted a perspective of crafting strategy, i.e. a line of thinking in which strategy formulation and implementation are no longer considered to be purely sequential processes.[3] Here strategy making is considered more an organic process that has both deliberate and emerging elements. Top-down and bottom-up influences interact shaping strategy.

Second marketing managers' adoption of the strategic management literature in the mid-1980s left them with a gap between the general business strategies that were formulated and the operational marketing mix activities employed. particularly affected, or better hindered, a smooth marketing implementation. Corporate and business plans tend to lack detail toward customers and filling in the marketing mix. Only since the late 1990s, when marketing strategy became more focused on segmentation and positioning, this problem has been overcome.[4]

Finally, the emergence of the market-oriented organization as a separate literature has fueled the awareness for market oriented culture as a key success factor resulting in a heightened attention for building market information systems and disseminating customer and competitor information throughout the organization.[5] The recognition that organizations should have market oriented cultures has helped managers focus on the organizational aspect of strategy *and* marketing. However, there is also a dark side to this development. Apparently some companies have become too customer-*led* and have developed a new form of marketing myopia resulting from following their customers blindly.[6] The lesson to be learned is that companies should both listen to their current and potential customers and remain critical trying to understand future market trends. The solutions and products developed should fit current *and* potential customers' needs. This may require educating customers for this purpose.

Gumesson argues that successful implementation of strategic marketing requires adopting *a relationship paradigm* between the company and its customers.[7] In order to be able to create customer value effectively managers should *really* understand their customers and future customers. This is more than doing business on a regular basis and being on good terms. It means understanding the customers processes and their definition of value, together with the future developments affecting the customers' situation. The traditional focus on the exchange process (e.g. buying behavior and motivations) should thus be substituted for a detailed inquiry into the *exchange and customer value creation process.* This requires an advanced customer and customer interface management. Generally this takes years to develop and should be an important objective for every marketing manager or director.

8.2.2 IMPLEMENTATION

Implementation deals with the allocation of means and mobilizing resources in accord with the corporate or business plan made. It also involves people management. The willingness, motivation and competence of the people in the organization are key to a successful implementation. The level of cooperation within the organization and the support of the organization's members for the strategic choices made depend to a large extend on goal congruity. An organization is a collective of people with collective, i.e. firm objectives. However, each member will also have his or her personal objectives. Function and department related objectives and points of view intermediate these collective objectives and personal objectives.[8]

In order to have good support within an organization and have a solid basis for change it is important that personal and collective objectives are consistent with or complement each other. When such consistency is failing departments or individuals may optimize for their personal goals rather than for the company's market position. Sub-optimization will then emerge and the organization will become less effective and efficient. In the worst case scenario even a political arena may emerge, introducing the end of the organization as it becomes more and more ineffective or paralyzed.[9] To prevent this from happening management may invest in formulating a broad but suitable mission statement for the company and communicate it actively to its members.

Although some authors have suggested that structure follows strategy, structure and other organizational characteristics such as culture and systems tend to cause inertia. Also the existing budget systems, allocation of means, control and reward systems may hinder change. Management can take several measures to stimulate a good organizational climate that supports strategy and joint action. This includes open communication, clear and well motivated decisions, operating performance systems that challenge people to improve the company's market position rather than to shirk or sub-optimize (e.g. improving one department's position), and encouraging cross functional teamwork and job rotation. Because most implementation problems are related to each other it is important to understand that actions in one area affect those in another. Therefore, it is important that the organization monitors its processes and learns from its mistakes in order to improve and keep improving its implementation process. A strong culture may facilitate implementation as members connect well because of shared values.

8.2.3 MARKETING AND MARKET ORIENTATION

Organization history and marketing's position in the company are two important factors affecting the implementation of marketing strategy. When the function is well developed and fully integrated in the organization it will be much easier to formulate strategic marketing ideas and execute a marketing plan creating customer value in the market place. This is why it is important as a manager to understand the evolution of the marketing function in companies and assess the situation in the company at hand. It will help to understand the barriers to implementation and help identify the challenge to further marketing in the organization.

Figure 8.1 shows the organizational life cycle and links it to environmental turbulence and product complexity. To understand the figure we first should focus on the horizontal axis. It represents the development of a company from its pioneering stage to its old age, as a full-fledged company. On the vertical axis we find the levels of development of the marketing function and the marketing department. The former relates to the degree to which marketing strategic and tactical activities are being developed and executed by the organization, whereas the latter refers to the physical presence of a marketing department in a firm. We can see from the graph that the marketing function and department have different "life cycles" in relationship with the organizational life cycle.

As a company develops, i.e. grows so will the marketing department and marketing function. First the emphasis will be on sales but as sales decrease due to a maturing market new customers and products will be needed for the firm to survive or continue to grow. Thus, a need for marketing evolves. As a result a marketing person or department will often be installed. However, to become really market driven the marketing function needs to diffuse into the organization. This is why over the past decade new product development has become more customer-oriented and sales management has evolved into account management. These trends have tended to reduce the size of the marketing department. As the marketing function spreads out in the organization and becomes more integrated the marketing department becomes smaller. It becomes a support task.

Of course the above is a simplification and generalization. Many companies will never leave the pioneer stage or are born as full-fledged companies. Nevertheless it gives us an idea of the general developments taking place and why some companies are more receptive than others to the marketing and market orientation paradigm.

When a company's products are more complex or when services are involved a stronger need to integrate marketing in the organization will be present. When the environment is more turbulent and competitive, an organization should also be more market-driven and thus be looking for a stronger market oriented culture. The reason is simple. When the marketing function is not very well developed and dispersed in the organization this may hinder marketing strategic change, i.e. flexibility. Particularly when the organization has a complex product and when the environment is turbulent, keeping track of changing customer needs and looking for new ways to better satisfy them is essential.

Figure 8.1: Distinguishing between the marketing function and the marketing department[10]

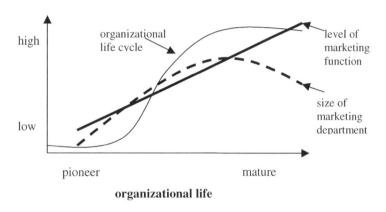

In conclusion, a large marketing staff is no evidence of good marketing. For this a more careful evaluation of the marketing function and the role of the marketing department is required.

8.3 THE CONTENT OF IMPLEMENTATION

Implementation consists of three core elements complementing each other (see Figure 8.2). These include: (a) building the organization capable of implementing the strategic marketing plan, (b) the actual implementation of the content of the plan to realize the new customer value, and (c) the evaluation and control of the organization's activities. Each element will be discussed below. We should, however, not consider the formulation and implementation of a marketing plan a sequential process, because it is not. It rather is an iterative and integrated process in which the different components influence each other. This is why the circles of figure 8.1 are drawn to overlap each other.

8.3.1 BUILDING THE ORGANIZATION

In a strategic marketing plan the new or additional customer value that the company is or will be aiming for is defined. Sometimes the firm's existing knowledge and facilities will be sufficient to create this new or additional value. Generally this is when business evolves slowly and gradually. However, sometimes a serious investment in skills, equipment and systems is needed, e.g. when a company is embarking on a new technology or completely new market. Therefore, the first step of implementation is to evaluate the firms' resource requirements in the light of the strategy adopted. For instance, when consumer electronic manufacturer Philips recognized that consumers had started to value product design more and Philips was not at par with competitors like Bang and Olufsen or Sony, it recognized that it needed more excellent designers next to good marketing and Research & Development staff. Apart from the "what" question, the amount and type of resources (design courses for current staff or hiring new designers) has to be addressed. In general it is not an individual resource that creates unique customer value but the unique combination of resources put together.

Figure 8.2: Components of implementation

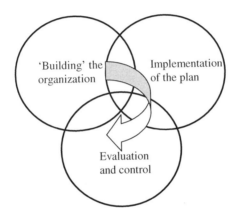

An important aspect to consider is the fit between the new resources and the firm's current resources. While trying to analyze and complement the company's resource situation management can and should fall back on the information generated through the internal analysis (see Chapter 4). Particularly the information from the *activity system analysis* has proven to be useful for understanding which resources (including systems) the organization should develop and how to fit them in its current operations. As a first step toward developing the organization and resource position the new activity system can be drawn. It can serve as a guideline also for the implementation process. The new resources may be related or unrelated resources (e.g. technology). The latter will create very different management issues. When unrelated resources are involved management should first learn about the possibilities and ways to integrate the new resources in the organization. Aspects like training and unlearning yesterday and inventing tomorrow should be explored to get a grip on the feasibility of adopting the resources successfully. Some kind of internal marketing program to "sell" the resources may proof helpful.[11]

8.3.2 EXECUTING THE ACTUAL PLAN

Before a plan can be executed several steps need to be taken. The marketing plan that has been formulated should be analyzed from a process perspective. This involves identifying activities/tasks and prioritizing them. Sometimes it is wise to cluster certain activities for reasons of convenience or with particular synergies in mind. Next, people should be assigned and a final planning can be made. The planning should calculate for activities that should be done first and those that can be done later. The easiest way is to make a graph capturing all the activities and plotting them against a time line (compare PERT-planning or critical path planning). Distinguishing between *short, medium and long-term actions* is a well established method that has proven to be very useful. Responsibilities, authority and means need to be specified.

Of course it is important to get the right man or woman for the job and make sure that the situation allows for his or her success (complementing responsibility with authority and providing adequate resources!). From a marketing perspective involving product management, sales and channel management, and those responsible for pre- and post-sale customer service will be most important.

Finally, management should check the overall feasibility of the plan both with regard to *stress and stretch* for the organization. Adequate cash flow needs to be ensured also. When the stress or stretch is too large the plan should be phased in, introduced under the creation of an external threat, or abandoned all together. However, it is important to let the company's marketing plan and "content-need" direct the implementation and not vice versa.

Learning from past experiences is an important part of any organization especially where implementation is concerned. Particularly large organizations can identify best practices and copy this throughout the organization making some adaptations to the circumstances at hand. For example, Unilever, the food and detergent company, has developed a roadmap for introducing supply chain and category management in a country based on experiences particularly in Northern Europe where large retailers demand such developments complemented with US trends. The roadmap now serves other subsidiaries in markets around the world to improve their "retail marketing".

8.3.3 EVALUATION AND CONTROL

To determine to what extend the company's marketing strategy and plan have been successful, the results should be monitored and evaluated. This information can then be used to modify the marketing effort if necessary and thus update the plan.

An evaluation consists of four steps:
1. First performance criteria have to be formulated. Generally the marketing objectives (as formulated in the strategic choice stage) and goals and objectives per marketing instrument (as formulated in the marketing program execution stage) will serve as

benchmark. As these goals tend to be quantitative in nature and have a deadline they are particularly well suited for evaluation purposes. The results can simply be confronted with the original goals and thus expectations. Additional criteria may be formulated for ease of implementation and organizational improvement. It generally makes sense to include an evaluation of each activity or task group separately and on a regular basis. Their direct contributions to sales and, more importantly, customer value, should be evaluated.

2. Next, management needs to gather data for each performance measure or criterion. The type of data and the timing for obtaining it will have to be established. A distinction can be made between:
    *   data from the internal organization itself such as financial data and sales figures from the sales department
    *   data from standard data services such as Nielsen market information (e.g. market share)
    *   data from particular and specifically executed studies, e.g. periodical customer satisfaction studies and customer loyalty studies
    *   data of continuously monitoring and scanning the environment

    For each category a planning regarding the data collection should be made. Monitoring day-to-day operations and strategic change will require different systems with different time horizons and data gathering/reporting cycles. Management should make sure that systems for both activities are in place.

3. Third, a careful analysis is required to establish the marketing program's quality. Management should not only identify the results but also look for the underlying causes of meeting or not meeting expectations. Of particular interest is the question whether deviations are caused by changes in the environment, poor plans or poor execution of these plans. The outcomes of the evaluations of tactical operations may be used as immediate feedback to help the execution of the marketing plan.

4. The final step involves the strategy audit. This involves an overall evaluation and a confrontation of the results with the marketing strategic objectives. The environmental trends will be included in the evaluation. Now adjustments can be made to the overall plan. The evaluation cycle used should depend on the level of turbulence in the environment and the degree of strategic modification or turnaround the organization is aiming for.

8.4 INSTRUMENTS TO USE

To help management manage the marketing effort several instruments are available. We made a small selection again. We start with a facilitating and general tool, i.e. the six-step roadmap developed by Day[12] to make an organization market oriented. Although it can not be used to implement a particular marketing plan it increases an organization's receptiveness for strategic marketing initiatives and activities. Next the Activity plan and Balanced Score Card (BSC) will be discussed.

8.4.1 MARKET ORIENTATION

Implementing marketing strategy is easier in a market driven than in an internally focused company. Market orientation's roots can be traced back to Peter Drucker and the growth of marketing after World War II. He suggested that each company should engage in marketing and place the customer first. "Marketing is not only much broader than selling, it is not a specialized activity at all. It is the whole business seen from the point of view of its final result, that is, from the customer's point of view"[13]. Consistent with this notion, market orientation has been defined as "the organization culture that most effectively and efficiently creates the necessary behaviors for the creation of superior value for buyers and, thus, continuous superior performance for the business".[14] Acquiring market information and dissemination of such information within the company are considered to be the key to a company's becoming market oriented. It is a prerequisite for a market driven culture. [15]

Day[16] identifies a six-step change program for companies to become market oriented, including:

1. Diagnosis of current capabilities
2. Anticipation of future requirements
3. Bottom-up-redesign of underlying processes
4. Top-down support and involvement for the changes
5. Introducing creative use of information technology
6. Introducing a continuous evaluation and control of the firm's market oriented behavior

The changes should increase the company's ability to monitor the market, act based on this information, and to better relate to customers. Characteristics of market driven organizations are active market scanning, a self-critical attitude toward benchmarking using front runners (in ones own or the area considered), and a continuous experimenting to improve products and processes.

Note that a customer orientation should not be limited to external customers and exchanges alone. It can also be applied internally, on internal exchanges of the company. This will facilitate internal processes and help organizational members to see their contribution to the added value the company is creating for customers.[17]

Top management and the marketing department should actively promote market orientation within the company. They are in a position to help build market information systems and disseminate the information from these systems promoting active use of the information. It will help increase the organization's market responsiveness. Importantly, it will help to create an (informational) infrastructure in which the implementation process will be facilitated.

8.4.2 ACTIVITY PLAN FOR THE COMMERCIAL FUNCTIONS

Activity planning is a tool for implementing a marketing plan, or in fact any plan. It involves translating a plan into a *set of activities* and complementing it with a time horizon, budgets and people (see Figure 8.3). It is closely related to tools such as PERT planning and critical path analysis. It represents a systematic way to address the following questions:

- Which tasks and activities need to be executed?
- How should they be performed?
- Who should perform them? Who is capable and in the position of performing them?
- Who should be made responsible and placed in control of their execution?
- When and where should the tasks be executed?
- Which type and size of budgets are required?
- Which organizational systems need to be developed and put in place?

Figure 8.3: Activity planning

Activities	People	Timing	Budget	Evaluation and Control
Identification of activities and tasks involved to realize the marketing plan	Identification of (a) project champion(s) and other people involved, including a specification of responsibilities and authority	Time frame for execution of the activities.	Financial means and allocation of means to execute the activities.	Program and time frame for evaluation and control. Ensure measurable outcomes.

Distinguishing between short and long-term and operational and strategic actions the different tasks of the project need to be identified. They are best plotted against a time line and in the right order identifying the critical path, i.e. those activities that can only start when others have been finished and are thus key to the continuation of the project. The critical path method holds the priorities because it distinguishes between things that should be done and may be done at a given point in time. Management can use the result to monitor the progress in execution and take action when the organization is falling behind schedule.

While implementing the marketing strategy, a major challenge is to overcome the (potential) barriers between the different departments or functional groups. Focussing on the commercial side of the organization Cespedes[18] identified the implementation barriers that emerge naturally from the differences between product management, sales/account management and customer service management. (see Box 8.2) Tools to counter the barriers include facilitating communications between them and building larger information systems that supersede the individual area and include the company level, job rotation and use of cross-functional teams (e.g. new product development, account teams). In line with this challenge not only individual performance measures should be formulated relating to one functional area. Measures covering more areas and particular those concerning cooperation and realizing synergies for value creation (the real core competencies) should be installed (e.g. evaluating an account team's performance based on improving the customers' level of improved strategic market position).

Box 8.2: Differences in information use, measurement systems and time horizons between commercial functions[19]

Marketing implementation barriers often reside in the information, measurement, and career path infrastructure of firms. Product managers, sales managers and customer service managers tend to differ in behavior on these three accounts, which may hinder the communication and understanding between these groups. A simple example we find in the joke that marketers know what should be sold next year while sales people are completely focused on today's sales.		
Below some major implementation differences between the three groups are identified:		
Product Management	**Field Sales**	**Customer Service**
Roles and responsibilities: Operate across geographical territories with specific product responsibilities.	*Roles and responsibilities:* Operate within geographical territories, with specific account assignments.	*Roles and responsibilities:* Operate within geographical territories, with multiple product/ account assignments.
Time horizons driven by: Product development and introduction cycles. Internal planning and budgeting processes.	*Time horizons driven by:* Selling cycles at multiple accounts. External buying processes.	*Time horizons driven by:* Product installation/maintenance cycles. Field service processes.
Key performance criteria: Performance measures based on profit/loss and market share metrics.	*Key performance criteria:* Measures based primarily on annual, quarterly or monthly sales volume.	*Key performance criteria:* Measures vary, but typically "customer satisfaction" and cost efficiencies.
Informat'n flows data priorities: Performance measures based on profit/loss and market share metrics.	*Data priorities:* Desegregated data about geographical markets, specific accounts and resellers.	*Informat'n flows data priorities:* Desegregated data about product usage at accounts.

Key data uses:	Key data uses:	Key data uses:
Roles of data makes compatibility with internal planning and budgeting categories a criterion of useful information.	Role of data makes compatibility with external buyers' categories important; "timely" data as function of varied selling cycles at assigned accounts.	Role of data makes compatibility with relevant technical vocabularies a criterion of useful information.
Information systems: Often incompatible with sales and service systems.	*Information systems:* Often incompatible with product and service systems.	*Information systems:* Often incompatible with product and sales systems.

A good activity plan lists all necessary activities and specifies the people involved or teams designed to do the job. Preferably specific projects with clear beginnings and endings are formulated with sub- goals and evaluations. Management should pay particular attention to how the different activities fit together and how each team or department contributes to the value creation for the customer. Further it should allow for bottom-up influence or adaptation of plans making market feedback and emerging strategy a serious part of the implementation. For this purpose it is good to pay particular attention to customer relationship management and educating customers to provide feedback systematically helping the company's market orientation and responsiveness.

Although the primary goal of the activity plan will be to accomplish the tasks at hand, i.e. those stemming from the strategic marketing plan, organizational learning is an important goal too. The organization may learn in two respects. First, regarding project management and implementation. Second, regarding the specific task and functional area at hand. For learning purposes it is important to document developments and the progress made. The project leader or champion is in a good position to evaluate the project after it has been ended and -also based on experiences with similar projects- formulate a best practices manual and road map.

Last but not least we should comment on the need for a clear financial evaluation and control of the plan. First, this should demonstrate that the plan is feasible. It should have adequate budgets that fit the objectives to be met. Simple checks are the communication (or product) goals and the communication (new product development) budget. Second, it should hold information on the bottom line. The plan should be profitable and clear about when it will break even. This should be proven using realistic growth figures in line with the marketing activities planned and the market situation at hand. It should be based on the market share objectives and market prices quoted, minus costs. Third, the plan should be clear the budgets for each marketing action or activity. When necessary it should have a budget for unforeseen costs. These budgets should be managed and controlled effectively, keeping track by monitoring the progress and costs made per activity/project.

8.4.3 BALANCED SCORE CARD

Initially introduced as a tool to broaden performance measures, the Balance Scorecard has evolved into a tool integrating and balancing different perspectives to effectively link strategic choice and organizational management; to link a company's long-term strategy with its short-term actions. The big advantage of the balance scorecard is coordination and integration. "senior executives [using it] discovered that the scorecard supplied a framework and thus a focus for many critical management processes: departmental and individual goal setting, business planning, capital allocations, strategic initiatives, and feedback and learning. Previously, those processes were uncoordinated and often directed at short-term operational goals. By building the scorecard, the senior executives started a process of change that has gone well beyond the original idea of simply broadening the company's performance measures."[20]

Figure 8.4 shows the instrument. It covers four areas, i.e. finance, customers, internal company processes and organizational learning. Depending on its situation, a company's management should select criteria from each area to monitor, evaluate and control its operations. Per area and criterion goals, intentions and actions need to be specified.

The content of the scorecard is company specific. While choosing the set of evaluation criteria management should try to balance between financial and customer-related criteria. Furthermore, the criteria should be in line with the company's vision, i.e. strategy. A cost oriented strategy will require more emphasis on efficiency measures whereas a differentiation strategy needs to pay more attention to customer effectiveness.

Critical steps in the execution of the balance scorecard are:
1. Clarifying the vision, i.e. strategy
2. Communicating it up and down the organization and linking it to departmental and personal objectives
3. Integrating business and financial planning, and
4. Feedback and stimulating strategic learning.

As financial aspects are easier to measure than business strategic aspects, there is a tendency to focus on hard, financial matters and to neglect the soft strategic and customer oriented ones. The result then is an unbalanced rather than a balanced scorecard. For a successful introduction management has to make sure that performance criteria of all four areas of the balanced scorecard and people of all departments are included. The latter is also in accord with our call for a market oriented organizational culture.

8.5 PRACTICAL GUIDELINES

We conclude this chapter with some practical guidelines that will help implementing the strategic marketing plan.

Figure 8.4: The balanced scorecard.

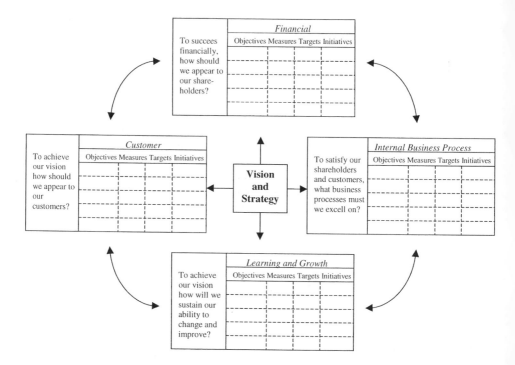

1. Note that developing the marketing function/department and the company's market orientation is an important aspect of implementation in general. Therefore, it makes a lot of sense to first perform a sound marketing audit focusing on this aspect. Based on the outcomes important implications for further developing the marketing function/department of the organization can be drawn. The result should be a concrete plan of action following Day's six-step roadmap.

2. Make sure that the marketing plan does not get implemented along the dimensions of departments. The guiding principle should be customer value creation and the relationship paradigm. The latter requires looking beyond borders and departments and creating teams focusing on customer value (product, service), customer cost (price, easy to use), convenience (delivery systems) and communication. These customer value components sometimes referred to as the 4 Cs of marketing[21] (see paragraph 7.3) are a good intermediary between the P's from the marketing mix and internal activities of departments.

3. Using a structured approach such as project planning (clear beginning and end, defining the project leader and his/her responsibilities and authority) is an easy and useful way of

defining activities. It will help the planning and control of activities. It will prevent that you forget important aspects.

4. With regard to the implementation of a marketing program, internal marketing, i.e. using the marketing philosophy on internal exchanges between departments and groups is a way to facilitate communicating the ideas to the organization and obtaining commitment from all involved.

5. Allow for a clear link between the decisions of implementation and the internal analysis of the organization made. This will ensure consistency in the marketing plan.

8.6 NOTES

[1] Nutt (1983)
[2] For a positive exception see Cespedes and Piercy (1996)
[3] See Bourgeois and Brodwin (1984) and Mintzberg (1987) respectively
[4] See e.g. Hooley, Saunders and Piercy (1998).
[5] Narver and Slater (1990).
[6] Gumesson (1998); Slater and Narver (1998)
[7] Gumesson (1998)
[8] Katz and Kahn (1966).
[9] Mintzberg and Westley (1992)
[10] Based on Homburg et al (1999)
[11] Hooley, Saunders and Nigel (1998).
[12] Day (1994).
[13] Drucker (1954).
[14] Narver and Slater 1990.
[15] See Kohli, Jaworski and Kumar 1993; and Deshpande and Farley 1998
[16] Day 1994.
[17] Hooley, Saunders and Piercy (1998).
[18] Cespedes (1993).
[19] Source: Cespedes (1993), p.29.
[20] Kaplan and Norton (1996).
[21] See Kotler (1999).

References

Abell, Derek (1980), *Defining the Business: The Starting Point of Strategic Planning*, Prentice Hall.

Adcock, Dennis (2000), *Marketing Strategies for Competitive Advantage*, John Wiley & Sons.

Anderson, James C. and James A. Narus (1999), *Business Market Management*, Prentice Hall.

Ansoff, H.I. (1965), *Corporate Strategy*, New York, NY: McGraw-Hill.

Ansoff, H.I. (1984), *Implanting Strategic Management*, Englewood Cliffs, NJ: Prentice Hall.

Argyris, C. and D.A. Schön (1978), *Organizational learning: A theory of action perspective*, Reading, MA: Addison-Wesley.

Barney, J.B. (1991), 'Firm Resources and Sustained Competitive Advantage', *Journal of Management*, 17 (1), 99-120.

Bijmolt, T.H.A., R.T. Frambach and Th.M.M. Verhallen (1996), 'Strategic Marketing Research', *Journal of Marketing Management*, Vol. 12, No. 1-3, p. 83-98.

Blake, R.R. and J.S. Mouton (1964), *The Managerial Grid*, Houston.

Bonoma, Thomas V. (1984), 'Making Your Marketing Strategy Work', *Harvard Business Review*, March-April.

Bourgeois, L. and D. Brodwin (1984), 'Strategic Implementation: Five Approaches to an Elusive Phenomenon', *Strategic Management Journal*, 5, p. 7-14.

Bunt, J., S. Wijnia and L. Kloosterman (1994), *Commercieel Management* [in Dutch], Groningen: Wolters-Noordhoff.

Business Week (1984), 'The new breed of strategic planner', September 17.

Campbell-Hunt, Colin (2000), 'What Have We Learned About Generic Competitive Strategy? A Meta-Analysis', *Strategic Management Journal*, 21, p. 127-154.

Cespedes, Frank. V. (1993), 'Coordinating Sales and Marketing in Consumer Goods Firms', *Journal of Consumer Marketing*, 10 (Summer), p. 37-55.

Cespedes, Frank V. and Nigel F. Piercy (1996), 'Implementing Marketing Strategy', *Journal of Marketing Management*, 12, p.135-160.

Choffray, Jean-Marie and Gary L. Lilien, *Market Planning for New Industrial Products*, New York: Wiley, 1980.

Clancy, Kevin J. and Robert S. Shulman (1991), *The Marketing Revolution*, New York, NY: Harper Business.

Coyne, K.P. and S. Subramaniam (1996), 'Bringing Discipline to Strategy', *McKinsey Quarterly*, 4, p. 14-25.

Cravens, David W. (1994), *Strategic Marketing*, Homewood, IL: Irwin.

Day, George S. (1990), *Market Driven Strategy*, New York, NY: The Free Press.

Day, George S. (1994), 'The Capabilities of Market-Driven Organizations', *Journal of Marketing*, 58 (October), p. 37-52.

Day, George S. and Robin Wensley (1983), 'Marketing Theory with a Strategic Orientation', *Journal of Marketing*, Vol. 47 (Fall), 79-89.

Day, George S. en Robin Wensley (1988), 'Assessing Advantage: a framework for diagnosing competitive superiority', *Journal of Marketing*, Vol. 52 (april), p. 1-20.

Doyle, Peter (1998), *Marketing Management and Strategy*, 2nd ed., Prentice Hall.

Drucker, Peter F. (1954), *The Practice of Management*, New York, NY: Harper and Row.

Engel, James F., Roger D. Blackwell and Paul W. Miniard (1986), *Consumer Behavior*, New York: Holt, Rinehart & Winston.

Ferrell, O.C., Michael D. Hartline, George H. Lucas Jr. and David Luck (1999), *Marketing Strategy*, The Dryden Press.

Frambach, R.T., E.J. Nijssen and H. Van Heddegem (1997). 'Industrial Pricing: Practices and Determinants in Two Sectors', in: Hartline and Thorne (eds.), *AMA Winter Educators' Conference Proceedings,* "Marketing Theory and Applications" - Volume 8.

Garbarino, Ellen and Mark Johnson (1999), 'The Different Roles of Satisfaction, Trust and Commitment for Relational and Transactional Consumers', *Journal of Marketing*, Vol.63 (April), p. 70-87.

Grant, Robert M. (1998), *Contemporary Strategy Analysis; Concepts, Techniques, Applications*, Oxford: Basil Blackwell.

Grove, Andy (1996), *Only the Paranoid Survive*, New York: Currency Doubleday.

Hamel, Gary (1998), 'Strategy innovation and the quest for value', *Sloan Management Review*, Winter, p. 7-14.

Hamel, Gary (2000) *Leading the Revolution*, Cambridge, MA: Harvard Business School Press.

Hamel,Gary and C.K. Prahalad (1994), *Competing for the future*, Boston: HBS Press.

Holbrook, Morris B. (1998) "Marketing Applications of Three-Dimensional Stereography", *Marketing letters*, Vol. 9 (Issue 1), p. 51-64.

Hill, T. and R. Westbrook (1997), SWOT Analysis: It's Time for a Product Recall, *Long Range Planning,* 30 (1), p. 4-5+46.

Hoes, Frank (1985), 'A Theoretical Framework for Integral Organization Analysis' [in Dutch], *Management en Organisatie*.

Homburg, Christian, John P. Workman Jr., and Harley Krohmer (1999), 'Marketing's Influence within the Firm', *Journal of Marketing*, Vol.63, Nr.2 (April), p. 1-17.

Hooley, Graham J., John Saunders and Nigel Piercy (1998), *Competitive Positioning* (2nd ed.), Prentice Hall.

Howard, John. A. and Jagdish N. Sheth (1969), *The Theory of Buyer Behavior*, New York: Wiley.

Hutt, Micheal D. and Thomas W. Speh (1995) *Business Marketing Management*, Fort Worth Texas: Dryden Press.

Jain, Subhash C. (1997), *Marketing Planning and Strategy*, South-Western.

Johnson, Gerry en Kevin Scholes (1997), *Exploring Corporate Strategy; Text and Cases*, Hemel Hempstead: Prentice Hall.

Kaplan, Robert S. and David P. Norton (1993), 'Putting the Balanced Scorecard to Work', *Harvard Business Review*, September-October, p. 134-142.

Kaplan, Robert S. en David P. Norton (1996), 'Using the Balanced Scorecard as a Strategic Management System', *Harvard Business Review,* January-February, p. 75-85.

Katz, D. and R.L. Kahn (1966), *The Social Psychology of Organizations*, New York, NY: Wiley.

Kim, W.C. and R. Mauborgne (1997), 'Value Innovation: The Strategic Logic of High Growth', *Harvard Business Review*, Vol. 75, No. 1, p. 103-112,

Kohli, Ajay K. and Bernhard J. Jaworski (1990), 'Market Orientation: The Construct, Research Propositions, and Managerial Implications', *Journal of Marketing*, Vol. 54 (April), 1-18.

Kotler, Philip (1999), *Kotler on Marketing; How to Create, Win, and Dominate Markets*, New York, NY: The Free Press.

Kotler, Philip (2000), *Marketing Management; analysis, planning, implementation and control*, 10th edition, Englewood Cliffs, NJ: Prentice Hall.

Lambin, Jean-Jacques (1993), *Strategic Marketing*, McGraw-Hill.

Lee, H.J. van der (1991), *Strategisch Management* [in Dutch], Samson.

Leeflang, Peter S.H. (1994), *Probleemgebied Marketing* [in Dutch], Educatieve Partners Nederland.

Markides, C. (1998), 'Strategic Innovation in Established Companies', *Sloan Management Review*, Vol. 39, No. 3, p. 31-42.

Mintzberg, Henry (1983), *Structure in Fives: Design of Effective Organizations*, Englewood Cliffs, NJ: Prentice Hall Inc.

Mintzberg, Henry (1987), 'Crafting Strategy', *Harvard Business Review*, September-October, p. 66-75.

Mintzberg, Henry (1988), *Mintzberg on Management: Inside our Strange World of Organizations*, New York: The Free Press.

Mintzberg, H. and F. Westley (1992), 'Cycles of Organizational Change', *Strategic Management Journal*, Vol.13, p. 39-59.

Morgan, Robert M. and Shelby D. Hunt. (1994), 'The Commitment-Trust Theory of Relationship Marketing', *Journal of Marketing*, Vol.58, (July), p. 20-38.

Narver, John C. and Stanley F. Slater (1990), 'The Effect of a Market Orientation on Business Profitability', *Journal of Marketing*, 54 (October), p. 20-35

Nijssen, Edwin, Jagdip Sing, Deepak Sirdeshmukh, with Hartmut Holzmueller, (2000) 'The Industry Context of Consumer-Firm Relationships: A Consumer Dispositions Approach for Examining its Impact and Implications', *Working Paper*, Case Western Reserve University, Weatherhead School of Management.

Nutt, Paul C. (1983), 'Implementation Approaches for Project Planning', *Academy of Management Review*, 8 (4), p. 500-611.

Penrose, Edith T. (1959), *The theory of the growth of the firm*, Oxford: Basil Blackwell.

Piercy, Nigel F. (1998), 'Marketing implementation: The implications of marketing paradigm weakness for the strategy execution process', *Journal of the Academy of Marketing Science*, 26 (3), p. 222-236.

Porter, Michael E. (1980), *Competitive Strategy: Techniques for Analyzing Industries and Competitors*, New York: The Free Press.

Porter, Michael E. (1985), *Competitive Advantage: Creating and Sustaining Superior Performance*, New York: The Free Press.

Porter, Michael E. (1996), 'What is Strategy?', *Harvard Business Review*, Vol. 74, No. 6 (December), p. 61-80.

Prahalad, C.K. and G. Hamel (1990), 'The Core Competence of the Corporation', *Harvard Business Review*, Vol. 68, May/June, p. 79-91.

Roest, H. and W. Reijnders (1999), *Cases Marketingstrategie* [in Dutch], Houten: EPN.

Rust, Ronald T., Anthony J. Zahorik and Timothy L. Keiningham (1996), *Service Marketing*, Harper Collins.

Schnaars, Steven P.(1991) *Marketing Strategy*, New York, NY: The Free Press.

Sidhu, J.S., E.J. Nijssen and H.R. Commandeur (2000), 'Business Domain Definition Practices: Does it Affect Organizational Performance?', *Long Range Planning* (forthcoming).

Singh, Jagdip and Deepak Sirdeshmukh (2000), 'Agency and trust mechanisms in consumer satisfaction and loyalty judgements', *Journal of the Academy of Marketing Science*, Vol. 28 (Winter), p. 150-167.

Stern, El-Ansary and Coughlan (1996) *Marketing Channels*, 5th edition, Englewood Cliffs, NJ: Prentice Hall.

Treacy, Micheal and Fred Wiersema (1995) *The Discipline of Market Leaders*, Reading, MA: Addison Wesley Publishing Company.

Van Waterschoot, Walter and Christophe Van den Bulte (1992), 'The 4P Classification of the Marketing Mix Revisited', *Journal of Marketing*, Vol. 56 (October), p. 83-93.

Webster, Frederick. E. and Yoram Wind (1972), A General Model for Understanding Organizational Buying Behavior, *Journal of Marketing*, Vol. 36 (April), p. 12-19.

Weick, K.E. (1979), *The Social Psychology of Organizing*, Reading, MA: Addison-Wesley.

Wernerfelt, Birger (1984), 'A Resource-Based View of the Firm', *Strategic Management Journal*, Vol. 5, p. 171-180.

INDEX